D1230771

296.714
SCH

Judaism:
Embracing
the Seeker

Wapiti regional library

Judaism: Embracing the Seeker

PAPL
DISCARDED

ᔐ

Introduction and Foreword by
RABBI HAROLD M. SCHULWEIS

Edited by
MICHAEL HALPERIN

KTAV PUBLISHING HOUSE, INC.
Jersey City, New Jersey 07306

Copyright © 2010 Valley Beth Shalom, a California non-profit corporation
All Rights Reserved

Library of Congress Cataloging-in-Publication Data

Schulweis, Harold M.
  Judaism : reaching out and embracing the seeker / Introduction and foreword by
Harold M. Schulweis ; edited by Michael Halperin.
    p. cm.
  ISBN 978-1-60280-141-7
  1. Judaism. 2. Jewish converts from Christianity. I. Halperin, Michael. II. Title.
  BM45.S443 2010
  296.7'14--dc22
                        2009048410

Published by
KTAV Publishing House, Inc.
930 Newark Avenue, Jersey City, N.J. 07306
www.ktav.com
Email: orders@ktav.com
Phone: 201-963-9524 • Fax: 201-963-0102

Let Your tender mercies be stirred for the righteous, the pious, and the leaders of the House of Israel, devoted scholars and faithful Jews by choice. Be merciful to us of the House of Israel. Reward all who trust in You; cast our lot with those who are faithful to You. May we never come to despair, for our trust is in You. Praised are You, Adonai, who sustains the righteous.

We appreciate the generosity of
Lori and Ron Freson
which enabled the publication of this journal.

ب

We gratefully acknowledge the following individuals
for their gifts of energy and spirit in the creation of this journal:

Jane Jacobs
Debbie Shayer
Elana Zimmerman

ب

Counselors:
Rabbi Edward Feinstein
Rabbi Joshua Hoffman
Rabbi Paul Steinberg
Rabbi Noah Zvi Farkas
Cantor Herschel Fox
Cantor Phil Baron

Contents

PART TWO — THE CHALLENGE, THE HOPE, THE JOY: REACHING OUT TO THE WORLD

POEMS

Introduction

THE YOUNG MAN CAME to see me about adopting Judaism as his way of life. He was a spiritual seeker and he had learned and studied about Jewish history, Jewish literature, Jewish ethics and Jewish observance. But he said that something was lacking.

"What was lacking?" I asked him. And he answered with one word: "Ancestry."

"I need to find," he said, "something in my genealogy, some great-great-great Jewish grandparent, and that will confirm my conviction that I can become a Jew."

I told him that I respected his search, but added that this was not, to my mind, the essence of Jewish identity. For the pride we have in those who become Jews is in their freedom of choice. They are not Jews by blood type, but by character type. They are Jews because they have found in Judaism wisdom, ethics, a style of life and a sense of the future that will fulfill their yearnings to become reflective of the image of Godliness. Judaism is not a matter of race and it is not a matter of "pure blood." We do not choose our DNA. We choose our character.

They have chosen without coercion and without ulterior motive. They have chosen to identify with a common fate and faith. They have come to our tradition from out of earlier religious traditions or lack of religious traditions. They come as mature people, aware that Jews are not a perfect people and that Judaism is great not because it is infallible, but because it is corrigible. Throughout our history, we have eliminated that which was unfit and added that which made us greater in the eyes of God.

They recognize that the rabbi is not a sanctified being, more privileged than any layman. The rabbi is human. And they have been taught that they understand there is no one who has done good on the face of this earth and has not transgressed.

My friend who came to me during his search understands the great emphasis upon the family, ethics and the service to humanity that is inherent in Judaism. Jewish belief and practice can only be authenticated by the individual. Joining our people does not depend on tracing a genealogy or ancestry, but by following the heart, soul and mind.

When taken seriously, are we not all Jews by choice? Our history ennobles us, our teachings enrich us, but we are Jews because we have chosen Judaism.

The great philosopher Hermann Cohen wrote, "In the stranger, man discovered the idea of Judaism." In the stranger, we have discovered ourselves.

H.M.S.

Foreword

To our Growing Jewish Family

W<small>E ARE A FAMILY</small>, a growing family, with an increasing number of Americans not born or raised as Jews seeking to join us. We enthusiastically welcome Jews by choice who seek to identify themselves with our community of faith. Through choice, new Jews are *mishpachah.* ·

Yet there are some who oppose opening the gates to non-Jewish spiritual seekers. They live with the misleading myth that proactive conversion of non-Jews is contrary to the principles and practices of Judaism. This myth has cast a large shadow over the *mitzvah* of conversion.

Some have forgotten that the first Jew by choice was the founder of Judaism. Abram, descended from pagan ancestors, is mandated by God to get out of his native land and father's house. "I will make of you a great nation, and I will bless you. I will make your name great, and you shall be a blessing. I will bless those who bless you and curse him that curses you; and all the families of the earth shall bless themselves by you" (Genesis 12:2–3).

We are not a people determined by race, but a living organism defined by voluntary choice.

Judaism's birth came through conversion. According to rabbinic tradition, Abram and Sarai sought converts and, through their efforts, God became known as Sovereign of the earth as well as Sovereign of the heavens. Who was there for Abram and Sarai to make into a people except the pagan non-Jewish populous around them? The Passover *Seder* that celebrates the birth of our people reminds us that our ancestors were idolaters, strangers and slaves.

Not our births, but our becoming identifies our being. Not the origin of ancestry, but the character of our progeny defines us.

On the festival of Shavuot, which celebrates the revelation of the Law, the rabbis selected the Book of Ruth to be read to the congregation. Ruth was a Moabite woman, and in accordance with the Torah, a Moabite was prohibited marriage to a Jew (Deuteronomy 23:4). Nevertheless, it is Ruth as a proselyte who is revered as the great-grandmother of King David, from whom the Messiah is said to spring. The rabbis proudly claimed others as Jews by choice: Bityah, the daughter of Pharaoh; Jethro, the father-in-law of Moses; Zipporah, the wife of Moses; and Shifrah and Puah, the Egyptian midwives who refused to obey the edict of Pharaoh to drown Jewish males and thereby saved Jewish lives.

In a Talmudic passage (*P'sachim* 87b), we read that the exile of Jews from their homeland served to increase the number of converts to Judaism, which itself is a glory to God. The honor due to converts finds expression in the 13th benediction of the 18 benedictions of the daily *Amidah*: We praise God for the "righteous proselytes" (*geirei tzedek*) who are a blessing to us and to God.

How then did the myth spread that Judaism is indifferent to or opposes conversion?

The distinguished Jewish historian Salo Baron pointed out that 2,000 years ago, Jews were 10 percent of the Roman Empire and had increased their numbers from 150,000 in 586 B.C.E. to 8 million in the first century C.E. Conversion to Judaism was hugely successful in those days and Jews worked hard to convert pagans, as the Gospel of Matthew testifies when referring to Jewish proselytizers who travel over sea and land to make a single proselyte (Matthew 23:15). This historically documented proactive outreach to non-Jews was put to an end not because of the proscriptions of Judaism, but because of the harsh edicts of the Roman emperors, especially Domitian and Hadrian who ruled Jewish proselytism to be a capital crime. In 313 C.E., the Roman emperor Constantine declared Christianity the state religion of Rome and declared that whoever joined "the nefarious sect" of Judaism would be burned alive. Such laws were incorporated in the *Codex Theodosianus*. It was not Judaism then that prohibited the prose-lytization of non-Jews, but the edicts of Hadrian that silenced the prose-lytizers.

In the 12th century the Jewish philosopher and codifier Moses Mai-monides was asked by Obadiah whether he, as a convert to Judaism, could recite such prayers as "Our God and God of our fathers." Maimonides responded forcefully: "By all means you should pray 'Our God and God of our fathers,' for in no respect is there a difference between us and you. Do not think little of your origin. If we trace our descent from Abraham, Isaac and Jacob, your descent is from Him by whose words the world was created."

The sociologist Gary Tobin recently appealed to the Jewish commu-nity, "Open the gates to all those who might choose to become Jews— opening the gates means embracing proactive conversion which is the open, positive, accessible and joyful process of encouraging non-Jews to become Jews" (*Opening the Gates*, 1999).

The gates are open. To the spiritual seekers who would enter the gates of Judaism, let the synagogue open its portals wide and welcome our growing family of inherited history and faith.

Who are they who join our ranks? They are neither surrogates for lagging birth rates nor replacements for our Holocaust losses. They are serious men and women who have searched their hearts and minds and chosen to attach themselves to our family. They contribute to the en-hancement of our spiritual life and, in turn, are deepened through the wisdom and values of the tradition of our family.

The Talmud observes that the biblical precept to understand and "love the stranger" refers to the proselyte. The Scripture's imperative to love the stranger appears no less than 36 times throughout the Bible. The stranger in our midst is the mirror reflection of our own selves. Enveloping the stranger, we embrace ourselves. A text in Leviticus 19:34 sums up the history, theology and morality of embracing the proselyte: "The stranger who sojourns with you shall be with you as the home born, and you shall love him as yourself for you were strangers in the land of Egypt: I am the Lord your God."

Out of personal experience I can testify to the dedication of those men and women who have studied text and prayer and found their spiritual fulfillment in Judaism. We are a choosing people and are blessed by those who mindfully unite themselves with our collective destinies.

I am indebted to Michael Halperin—a distinguished author, playwright and congregant—who has generously edited this personal journey. With him, I invite you to share the private journeys of our old-new family. The four meditations I wrote were inspired by my encounters with the spiritual seekers who have found their home.

Rabbi Harold M. Schulweis
Valley Beth Shalom, Encino, California

Discovering Judaism

We have asked
What you see in Judaism.
What in classes of instruction and in experience
Has attracted you to this people
And this faith?
You have instructed us.

I have been drawn to Judaism for many reasons.
And in no order of importance.
    I discovered the celebration of inquiry, the dignity of the question,
    the sadness over the fourth son
    who does not even know how to ask.

I found in Judaism the liberating absence of dogma,
    apodictic authoritarian responses,
    answers that will tolerate no question.
I am moved by the humility of the religious leaders
    who for all their erudition lay no claim to infallibility,
    but know that they, like all who walk the face of the earth,
    are errant souls.

No saints, unblemished, perfect, but even as our patriarchs and priests
    flawed and fallible
    struggling spirits.

In Judaism I found the enlarging embrace of inclusion.
    No faith, no race, no ethnicity excluded from the circle of salvation.
    No alien kept outside the circle, consigned to hell and perdition.
    Not souls, but lives are we mandated to save.

I am drawn to the faith that does not see sin inherited,
    an original stain on the heart of the newborn
    indelible sin that may not be erased by repentance, repayment, repair.

Injuries there are, not visited by ancestors upon our innocence
    but done to others and to ourselves
    would be healed and made whole,
    injuries for which I bear responsibility
    the capability to repair.

I am attracted to the inextricable bond between belief and behavior.
Faith demonstrated
>   not with the declarations of my mouth,
>   but with arms and legs.
>   Believing and behaving the twin duties of the heart.

In Judaism I find the focus on family,
>   the matrix of human relationships,
>   *mishpachah* around which the community revolves.

Choosing faith I choose family
And in its history and literature I find my family album.

I find in Judaism my own inner self.
My choice of Judaism is not burial of my past,
>   but recovery of some hidden treasures within.

I have long felt its vague presence, but never seen its face.
At long last, I have found the mirror that reflects the veiled,
>   concealed soul.

Rabbi Harold M. Schulweis

PART ONE

Why I Am A Jew

"*Throughout life one asks the same question in many forms. This question lies at the heart of a search for oneself, a search that begins with the first glimmer of consciousness and continues to the very last breath. For every human being it varies, and at every stage of his life. Often the search is conducted without any intellectual comprehension of what one is about. Sometimes the subtlest philosophical nuances of thought and speculation may be brought into play, and at others the question does not even rise to consciousness. But one never really extricates oneself from the context of the issue: Who am I? And from its corollaries: Where do I come from? Where am I going? What for? Why?*"

Adin Steinsaltz
The Thirteen Petalled Rose

I HAD MY FIRST BRUSH with Jewish culture in the second grade, in Bayonne, New Jersey, when a boy in my class bragged about the new watch he received on Hanukkah. He said he got a new present for each of the holiday's eight days. What restless, impatient 7-year-old who just found out Santa Claus is a fairy tale wouldn't be green with envy?

Not long after, we moved to Shoshone, California, where my father became district superintendent and principal of the Death Valley Unified School District. I began to see that some of the spiritual values I learned at home did not coincide with what was taught in Sunday school. Later, I attended a fundamentalist Baptist summer school where they told us that good Christians had to carry a Bible under their arm at all times and spread the word of Jesus at every opportunity. Since my parents did not approve of proselytizing, that was the last time I went to summer Bible school.

At 13, my parents sent me off to a church-affiliated summer camp. I was not prepared for the lack of physical activity and a bombardment of simplistic doctrines. Most of our time was spent in prayer meetings and lectures, usually about what we now call "intelligent design" or some other primitive Christian doctrine devoid of scientific reason.

I overheard one counselor commiserating with another because her son wanted to go to a secular university rather than the local Bible college. The other counselor frightened her with stories of young people who lost their religion in such dreadful places. I wanted to put as much distance between myself and this religion as possible. At the end of the week, I was the only one of more than 200 teenagers who had not declared herself "born again."

As a high school freshman, I wrote a report on the world's five religions. I also read a version of *The Greatest Story Ever Told* and *The Meaning of the Dead Sea Scrolls*. I had questions that revolved around the literal interpretations of the Bible.

Shoshone is probably one of the last places you would expect to meet Jews. My eighth-grade teacher's wife was Jewish. She taught part time and ran the high school library. She and my mother exchanged daytime baby-sitting duties since her daughter was the same age as my baby sister and both women worked part time. As I grew older, I spent more time with her. I was affected by her intense reaction to the Six-Day War. I was inspired to read *Exodus* and *The Diary of Anne Frank*. Though I haven't seen or heard from her in many years, she is still my model.

I met my future husband, Harris, in my senior year of college. Early in our relationship, I mentioned that I had an attraction to Judaism. Harris laughed, probably because I didn't have a clue what I was talking about.

After graduation, Harris and I worked in the apparel industry where we met a lot of the same people. I existed in a world of Jews and wanted very much to feel included. Over the next few years, I mentioned to friends and family that I planned to convert. Harris' family was generally very warm and friendly to me, but they became serious and stern when one of us mentioned my intention. Harris was told not to influence or pressure me. He gave me no encouragement and little support. He would not accompany me to *Shabbat* services to see what they were like. I put off the conversion process for several years and busied myself with work and outside classes. I was only moderately interested in a quest for spiritual identity and doubted I would find it in any organized religion.

In the meantime, we found a very liberal Reform rabbi, who performed a somewhat traditional wedding service. Our wedding was very small and only a few members of Harris' family attended. My mother knew Harris was Jewish. However, I'm not sure if she told my father. I didn't have the guts to tell him. Since they had moved to Texas, I felt quite detached from them. I don't think they were surprised or disappointed that I didn't invite them to the wedding.

Shortly after the wedding, our best friend began dating a store-buyer. She wanted to get married and told us she was taking classes on converting to Judaism at what is now American Jewish University. About that time, Harris and I began talking about starting a family. I was two-months pregnant when the next session of classes began. I enjoyed the study very much. Students were expected to attend services at various synagogues. We attended Friday night services at Reform temples and tried a Conservative synagogue where the vibrant sermon had to do with family values and contemporary issues. The large number of younger couples energized me and Harris introduced me to a friend he knew from business. We had found a home.

I went to a *mikvah* and a week or so later we had a group conversion. The arrival of our daughter postponed our official Jewish wedding ceremony. But we did it later, along with the baby naming, in front of Harris' parents.

My parents separated and divorced months after my daughter's birth and we drifted apart. I thought of my family as the most stable and steadfast family around, and I don't know what happened.

My daughter started Jewish day school and we joined a *havurah*. I learned more about Judaism culturally and sometimes spiritually through the *havurah*. The rabbi discussed the meaning of prayers and petitions to God. I was shocked to hear a rabbi say that the High Holiday prayers for another year of life should not be taken literally. The understanding began to sink in and I feel that I now have a much more adult understanding of the text.

Our children are both grown up and now I have time to study Talmud and am a great admirer of my teacher's contemporary approach. I may yet go for the gold: the adult *bat mitzvah*.

EACH TIME A PIECE OF MAIL arrives from my synagogue talking about a Jew-by-choice issue, I always think to myself, "That's interesting." Then I quite forget that the letter is talking about me.

My religious journey began with my baptism at 5 in the Presbyterian Church. I remember the passing of the offering plate and the "grape-juice" communion. When I was 12, my mother converted to the Episcopal Church where the communion wine was the real stuff and no longer grape juice. Throughout my teens, I argued with my mother whenever she tried to bring me to church. I didn't want to go even though I considered myself spiritual. I believed in God and prayer, but I had issues with the concept of Jesus and Easter was my least favorite holiday.

I had two best friends during my high school senior year. One was a devout Catholic, the other a born-again Christian. Both wanted me to join their faith.

Off to Catholic services I went and heard the priest announce that you could not pray at a mountain stream. This did not sit well with me because I felt closest to God at the top of a mountain, by the ocean or even on a thousand–year-old street in London.

Off to a Christian youth group meeting with my other friend, where a youth leader announced that we needed to go forth and tell 10 strangers about Jesus. That didn't feel right because I did not like talking to strangers, much less proselytizing them.

College introduced me to Jewish students and in the fall quarter I met and started dating the man I would eventually marry. I called my mother and told her I had a boyfriend and asked if it was all right that he was Jewish. She said of course. Thus began five years of large family gatherings around Rosh Hashana and Passover dinners, walking to synagogue in 100-degree weather for Yom Kippur and trying to explain to my mother why we cannot eat corn syrup for a week in the spring. (After 20 years, she still has problems understanding this one.)

The more I learned, the more I liked Judaism because it seemed to have the structured religious trappings that fit around what I already believed.

Several close friends were deeply religious Christians who told me that God was leading them and they thanked God for showing them the way. One had a son heading to Iraq and she calmly informed me that God would take care of him. The concept of a predestined plan bothered me. I prefer and embrace Judaism's notion that God made us in His image and I should emulate His guidance. I like the idea of personal responsibility. It just makes sense to me.

With my rabbi's help, the conversion process was easy. I studied! Then, after a *mikvah*, the rabbis and cantor interviewed me. I said the *Shema* before friends and family, and then I was Jewish.

My real challenge arose because I viewed religion separate from my life. I went to church on Easter and Christmas. I said grace only over Thanksgiving and Christmas dinners. Before my conversion, religion was just a title. Being Jewish felt not only like a title but a culture that seeped into every second of my life, changing the food I ate, the way I acted, the way I celebrated. Being Jewish was daily. It takes place in the home even more so than in the synagogue. How was I, a true WASP with a 230-year history in America, suddenly going to be "Jewish"? Woody Allen movies are not about my in-laws who are Sephardic Moroccan Jews. I consider myself Sephardic and will take couscous over gefilte fish every time. My experiences with Judaism had little in common with the stereotypical idea of Judaism.

The early years of my marriage resembled the earliest part of my life. I went to synagogue on the High Holidays, enjoyed the occasional *Shabbat* meal and once had the pleasure of organizing a Passover *Seder* for a dozen medical students. We found the *afikomen* three months later behind some books on a shelf. Evidently, twenty-somethings forget to search for it. Aside from the medical school *Seder*, my husband and I have spent every Passover for the last 28 years at my in-laws' house.

I realized that I might not be Jewish enough after giving birth to my second son during the High Holidays. My hospital records read "Jewish," so in came the rabbi in full Orthodox regalia holding an *etrog* and *lulav*. He started shaking the *lulav* around me and I stared in wonderment and a bit of astonishment. I had never seen a *lulav*, much less had one shaken around me while recovering from a challenging birth experience.

My recommendation to anyone wanting to convert to Judaism and be completely assimilated is to become a nursery-school teacher in a Jewish preschool. That's what I did. That and raising my children in Jewish preschool, Jewish day school and Jewish high school environments completed my immersion in Jewish culture and religion. I have taught for many years, and the highlight of my experience was teaching and sharing Jewish holidays with children. When you talk about *Lag B'Omer* with expertise, you know you arrived.

My biggest challenge was coming to terms with Christmas and Hanukkah. In my husband's youth, he celebrated Hanukkah with simple candle lighting and *gelt*. Maybe a present was given if anyone remembered. It was hard letting go of the magic of Christmas and it took 10 years before I came to peace on the subject.

Over time, a tradition has begun that looks remarkably like something from my childhood. On one night each Hanukkah, our family gathers to open presents as candles are burned and *latkes* are served. The most important aspects of holiday traditions are in full force: love and family.

Now that my children are in college, I have become a true Jewish mother. Are they dating Jewish girls? Will they keep the ethics, values and traditions we tried to instill in them? Are there too many blondes at the University of Arizona? Do they recognize that if they marry outside the faith, 2,000 years of tradition will be lost? Do they understand the perils of trying to raise children in a household of more than one religion? I always have a pinch of worry surrounding this issue.

I went searching for a religion that fit my needs and helped me make sense of the world. I found a religion that enriched my life and added value to it. I received even more than I was looking for. Since I converted, how could I be angry with my children if they search for something that fulfills their needs – and it does not happen to be Judaism? Would it be hypocritical to not allow them to convert as well?

My husband has given me the greatest gifts: himself, his unconditional love and his wonderful, magical, meaningful religion. I am blessed that my rabbi welcomed me with open arms and let me step into the warmth and richness that is the Jewish tradition. What's next? A visit to Israel, of course!

I had been dating my husband for only two years when my mother-in-law said randomly to him in front of me one day, "You are going to marry a nice Jewish girl." At the time, still exploring the world of Judaism, I felt hurt. Did she not want him to marry me? Years after my wedding, I teased her about this comment and she said simply, and with love, "He *did* marry a nice Jewish girl."

Prosper Benhaim

THE CONCEPT OF MARRYING someone not Jewish was a foreign concept as I grew up. I was 6 years old when I emigrated with my parents from Morocco. I witnessed their concerns about religion and potential retribution against Jews living in Morocco.

I grew up thinking that my family sacrificed so much to make sure life for their children was safer, better and free of religious strife. In that context, perhaps one not too dissimilar from other Jewish immigrant families from many corners of the world, it appeared rather unlikely that I would ever marry someone other than a Jewish woman.

I met Kathy during my freshman year of college and immediately recognized her as a genuinely kind, warm, funny and loving person – one with whom I rapidly fell in love. I remember thinking that I was a very lucky guy to have found someone so special. But as time went on, I worried about the logistics of how a mixed marriage would work when contemplating starting a family and raising children. It was probably through the initial exposure to my very loving family and its deep Moroccan Jewish traditions that Kathy first developed an interest in exploring Judaism. Kathy studied and accepted the Jewish faith with her usual enthusiasm and joy.

All members of my extended family, even the most deeply religious, recognize how Jewish Kathy is in every respect, and they fully embrace her as a treasured member of both our family and our rich religious tradition. She may not speak fluent Hebrew or read from Torah with ease, but her morals, warmth, generosity and unselfishness embody the absolute best of what Judaism represents. I could not be more proud of anyone.

Margaret & David Wininger

WE SUPPORTED OUR DAUGHTER KATHY when she decided to convert to Judaism. She married into a wonderful Jewish family and we have enjoyed all of the traditions and celebrations of the Jewish faith. We are especially impressed with the Jewish education our grandsons received at a Jewish day school and at the Jewish community high school. They were well-prepared for the colleges they chose as well as for life in general.

Georgette Benhaim

O F COURSE every Jewish mother wants her son to marry "a nice Jewish girl," and I feel so blessed that Kathy lives every day with integrity, compassion, kindness and love. Since Day One, she has been an important and vital part of our family. Kathy brings something very special to Judaism. Over the years, Kathy has added a few of her own creative touches to our Sephardic ways of celebrating *Shabbat*, Sukkot and Hanukkah. But the best way I can describe what Kathy means to us is through my parents' eyes. They were extremely traditional, but their love for Kathy was so strong it knew no bounds. It didn't matter what the religion, it only mattered who you were. My parents always greeted Kathy with love, blessings and open arms. We love Kathy and we thank her for her love and support, at all times. *Kol hakavod*, Kathy.

Jason Benhaim

M Y MOTHER'S DECISION to convert to Judaism was one of the best things to ever happen to me. True, I wasn't yet a twinkle in anyone's eye at that point, but I certainly have been reaping the benefits my entire life. As a child I found myself in the enviable position of being able to celebrate Hanukkah while also participating in my maternal family's Christmas celebrations, sometimes on the very same night! This exposure to another faith from an early age was valuable not only because it vaccinated me against Santa-envy, but also because it provided me with some exposure to the religious world outside the Jewish "bubble" that surrounded me at the private Jewish schools I attended for most of my life. Not that I ever resented this Jewish "bubble." Indeed, I am eternally grateful for my Jewish education and upbringing—two more things that would not have been possible without my mother.

Furthermore, my mother's being a convert really makes our family unique among Jewish—well, among *all* families. Her original contributions to our Jewish traditions and celebrations are universally admired and appreciated. Also, my brother and I may very well be the only two people in the entire world who claim both Jewish Moroccan and Pennsylvania Dutch ancestors, which has got to be good for the gene pool.

More than anything, I admire my mother for having the courage and self-awareness to seek out a religion that truly suited her. Luckily for me, I think Judaism suits my brother and me every bit as perfectly as it suits her. In that way, I think she made the right decision for more than one person.

Joelle Asaro Berman

G IVE US ADULT CHILDREN of intermarriage a stake in the incredibly rich tradition that is our Jewish future. When it comes to labeling, Jews take the cake. We've invented a term for nearly every Jewish lifestyle. While I knew from an early age that I bore the "Reform" label, I wouldn't learn of my "interfaith" label until I was an adult working full time in the Jewish communal world.

As a child, nothing struck me as strange about having a non-Jewish parent. It was the norm; many of my friends came from mixed households. That's what happens in the condensed suburbs of New Jersey. People from different backgrounds inevitably cross paths and, in some cases, decide to raise families together.

In my case the cross-pollination occurred between a Sicilian mother, raised Catholic in Lodi, New Jersey, and a mélange of Eastern-European-descent father, raised Jewish in Fair Lawn, New Jersey. They met at the nearby college where they both held teaching positions.

During her own college years, my mother's devotion to Catholicism dissipated, despite an unwavering faith in God. Her biggest obstacle to raising her future children in a particular faith was not the religion itself, but her distrust of all organized religion. Conveniently, my father's twin brother is a rabbi, and for an entire year he and my father worked to dispel her fear, answering her searching questions until she felt comfortable enough to raise us as Jews. Soon enough she was hosting my baby-naming ceremony and driving me and my brother David to Hebrew school.

And so I grew up, becoming a *bat mitzvah* at a Reform synagogue, discovering my Jewish identity at a Reform overnight camp and spending many fun weekends at Reform youth group events. Never was I labeled as an "interfaith kid." Having a non-Jewish mother was merely a genealogical footnote.

Imagine my surprise, then, when I started working in the larger Jewish communal world and was almost instantly labeled and made to feel inferior for having a non-Jewish mother. According to some of these Jews, my father was among those "finishing Hitler's work" by marrying outside the faith and pushing the Jewish people closer to extinction. Entire organizations and large sums of money were being devoted to studying the impact families like mine were having on Jewish continuity. The message was clear: Despite our Jewish upbringing, patrilineal children like me needed to suck it up and convert if we wanted to be considered legitimate outside the Reform world.

These detractors remain oblivious to how an interfaith family with both parents committed to raising Jewish children works. My parents figured it out early in their marriage. They concocted a careful, deliberate recipe sure to yield children with strong Jewish identities: A heaping serving of holiday observances sweetened by the recitation of blessings every Friday night at *Shabbat* dinner, a good measure of Hebrew school, *bar/bat mitzvah* and a generous pinch of participation in informal Jewish activities – especially Union of Reform Judaism Joseph Eisner Camp in Great Barrington, Massachusetts, where I made lifelong friendships.

Nowadays, the Jewish elements of my identity are as deeply ingrained as the Sicilian identity that my mother worked to infuse throughout my childhood. At our third-grade "Around the World Food Fair," I wore my great-grandmother's dress from Sicily and my mother helped me serve homemade ravioli. David and I couldn't just watch *The Godfather* – afterward, my mother would expound on the history of the Sicilian mob, which formed, we learned, as a result of the persecution and hardship Sicilian immigrants faced when they arrived in this country. I also followed my mother's example in scoffing at waitresses who would say "ca-la-mar-i" instead of the dialectally correct "co-la-mad."

Still, I was a Jew, even as we ate a special meal with my mother's side of the family every year during the Feast of St. Joseph. I was a Jew, even as I hung ornaments from the Christmas tree in our living room. I was a Jew, a proud Jew at that, when both sides of my family – grandparents, aunts, uncles and cousins—stood at my side as I ceremonially signed my *bat mitzvah* certificate at my temple in Franklin Lakes, New Jersey.

I see now that this is ultimately my parents' biggest success—that I know exactly who I am: an American Jew of Sicilian heritage. And so, after wrestling with the interfaith label for the past several years, I now realize it means nothing to me except that I had a somewhat unique upbringing for an American Jewish girl.

That said, as someone who's worn the interfaith label, let me offer some observations. One: Accept the reality of interfaith families. Whether you like it or not, the next generation of Jews will count many non-Jews as their parents and many not-typically-Jewish ethnicities as part of their identity. Two: Welcome interfaith families. For every interfaith family that's weathered the storm of feeling unwelcome and disadvantaged, there are plenty who get lost in the flood. There's no chance for Jewish continuity unless we open the tent to them all.

And last: Count in adult children of intermarriage. Give us a stake in the incredibly rich and resilient tradition that is also our Jewish future.

Reprinted with permission of Reform Judaism magazine, published by the Union for Reform Judaism

ALMOST EVERY SUNDAY, my family and I attended Presbyterian services or I went to Sunday school. Our church gave me a sense of safety and security; a place to belong and feel wanted. As I grew older, I volunteered as an assistant Sunday school teacher and spent my mornings teaching art and singing songs with kindergarten children. What could be better? My father was a deacon and quite popular on Sunday mornings. On Sundays, we were the perfect Christian family.

In college, I was recruited into a Christian movement. But the more I read and studied, the more I felt disconnected from the Christian world. Perhaps it highlighted the hypocrisies in my life or a sense of confusion, but Christianity no longer gave me the answers that I wanted to find. So I put religion on the "back burner" while I focused on my professional studies and goals.

I got married right out of college to a classmate who called himself a "partly Jewish atheist" and did not practice Judaism. As time went on, we grew apart and divorced. I threw myself into my profession and began to travel. I read extensively about other cultures and religions and developed ideas on how I wanted to live, what I valued and where I fit into the universe. I still did not connect to any particular religion, but became intrigued with my readings regarding Jewish thought. A trek to the top of Mount Sinai and discussions with tour partners reinforced my interest in and focus on Judaism.

Shortly after, I met the man who became my husband and life partner, Carl Blau. We spent hours discussing hypothetical events and how we would approach those experiences. Carl stated that he really wanted a Jewish home and to raise Jewish children. When I asked him what he meant, he responded by talking about holiday traditions such as Passover *Seders* and Yom Kippur "break-fasts." I knew that if I were to stay true to myself I would need a lot more out of this commitment. Carl and I started attending formal classes in Judaism.

We have been taking classes every year since that first Introduction to Judaism class. We started at a Reform temple and later moved to programs and membership at another temple in West Los Angeles, California. I continued studying and with each class felt closer to the words that I read. I connected very deeply to the Jewish sense of correcting a wrong. I believed in the pureness of a new child. I loved the sense of family connection and the history of Jewish traditions. My holidays felt empty for so long that finding the meaning in the *Seder*, the celebration of Sukkot, and the comfort of *Shabbat* and *Havdalah* made Judaism comforting. I greatly respected the guidance that Judaism offered.

I converted more than 17 years ago. Every time I welcome friends to our *Sukkah* or pass out spice bags for *Havdalah*, I am filled with such a sense of connection. Judaism inspires me to live my life in the best manner possible, to treat others with the same respect and to believe deeply in continuing to understand my purpose.

Sometimes I feel that I am bumbling my way through a maze of Jewish ritual. I wish I had a better understanding and a richer "vocabulary" when it comes to Jewish practices. I do think that learning about Judaism as an adult provides a different perspective, but at times I secretly wish that my actions came out of a more natural inherent understanding.

I am not always sure about people's reactions to my conversion. At times, I get the sense that people think I am not really Jewish because I converted. At the beginning of my search, I felt very awkward and not many people welcomed me. As each year passes, it gets easier because many people who I meet now hardly believe I converted. My adult *bat mitzvah* assured me it was true. As I participate in temple activities, I now find the sense of belonging that comes with familiarity. So perhaps I sing off-key or scramble for the right words, but I do feel this is "home."

My greatest joy as a Jew by choice has been watching my two daughters, Sarah and Emily, embrace the traditions of Judaism. I believe I have given them a gift far greater than they can understand and one that will support them throughout their lives. They have also inspired me to keep learning and growing into my role as a Jewish woman. I hope that I will inspire them to always question and search for new and deeper meaning in their own lives.

Lisa Bock

THIS IS A LOVE STORY. I fell in love with Ken, his family, his way of life and his extended family, including his temple family. His identity as a Jew has always been part of him—not that he really knew it—but I saw it and loved what I saw. His family was warm and welcoming, and they wrapped me into their family activities and celebrations.

Ken knew things about the Bible that I did not know, but had always wanted to know. He thought about God, but told me he honestly struggled, assuring me that as far as he knew it was perfectly fine to do so. He taught me that in Judaism there was no intermediary between an individual and God, and no need to be "saved." Doing the best you can in the world and for the world is all we know. After this life is over what is next is not known.

Those thoughts and ideas resonated with what I felt already. I found my home and my people. After years of wandering I came home.

Can someone fall in love for life at 15? Well, we say yes—we were just fifteen when we met. Somewhere along my journey, I learned the word *beshert*, "or meant to be," and that seems to be appropriate in describing not only my husband and me, but also my Jewish journey.

I feel so fortunate to have met Ken and to have started my Jewish journey at such a young age. I feel as though I've always been Jewish, only my parents didn't know it. I do miss not growing up with all the Hebrew songs and letters and I didn't go to camp. I feel as though I am always "catching up."

Ken Bock

WHEN I FIRST MET LISA, she was eager to learn about the Jewish religion. I attended classes with her to learn about Jewish culture and religion. As she continued to learn and move toward conversion and community involvement, she surpassed me in Jewish knowledge as well as participation.

To her credit, Lisa did not pressure me to be more than I wanted. She insisted that the kids get a Jewish education and I was happy to have her take the lead. She would become involved in spiritual and social Jewish life, and I would pursue a life of social activities in the community.

I am very proud of her growth as a person, for pursuing her passion and her involvement with others. I no longer feel left behind because it was never a race. It's the journey that matters.

Joanna Brent

GROWING UP IN THE 1940S in Toronto, Ontario, my immigrant Macedonian parents had a small "restaurant," really a glorified hot dog/hamburger stand.

The Goldbergs owned a dry-goods store next door. One day, my playmate Rosy did not come out to play, so I went upstairs to her family's apartment to ask about her. I found Mrs. Goldberg sitting at the table in a darkened room with a burning candle before her. She had her head in her hands, as if in distress, and would not reply to my questions. To this day I can still feel the sense of such overwhelming grief, an almost physical presence of awe. This occurred in the early years of the war. Had she learned some terrible thing about happenings in Europe? Could it have been Yom Kippur? Whatever it was, for me it seemed a vision of something powerful and compelling.

I remember going to the movies with my older sister and watching a newsreel and seeing fighting and turmoil and hearing the word "Israel" for the first time. I recall feeling that I was watching something being born, struggling to exist. I had no point of reference yet it affected me profoundly, as if something deep inside me was reaching out. But I was Macedonian, baptized in the Eastern Orthodox Church, the child of ordinary, run-of-the mill anti-Semites.

I left home at an early age to make a new life for myself. I met Nick, a Rumanian and a Jew. I felt at ease with him and sensed a trust that I had not experienced before. It was as if I had found a home at last. Nick was not raised with any *Yiddishkayt* at all. In fact, he, his family and his old Rumanian friends all denied their Jewish roots. Nick was opposed to any religious trappings but Quebec banned civil marriages. Therefore a Unitarian ceremony was as close as we could come to a nonreligious rite.

After 11 years, Nick and I parted. Eventually I met and married Barre, who was Jewish, but not observant. With Barre came his daughter Missy.

In her late teens, she met a young, very religious Moroccan from a family with an illustrious ancestor, a renowned *rebbe*.

Missy went through a conversion to marry this young man and Barre was furious and totally non-supportive. I was very close to Missy and understood her attraction. A child of divorce, she wanted structure and family and faith. Her struggle with her father brought us even closer and to this day I feel she's my daughter. My marriage to Barre lasted 10 years.

Finally I met Bob and we decided to marry. I said it was time for me to make a full commitment in every way. I wanted to convert to Judaism and marry properly. I took the superb course at what is now American Jewish University, joined a synagogue and had a beautiful garden wedding with a rabbi in the presence of all my wonderful Jewish friends and family – including Missy, her husband and two sons. Twenty wonderful years have passed, and I am truly home and blessed.

Rodney Burgoyne Jr.

I NEVER MET A JEW until I was around 15 years old. My family's attitude toward Judaism came out of Mormon theology. To some Mormons, Judaism was considered a brother religion that also suffered from pogroms. Judaism was given respect as the senior member in the religions of the Western world.

Christmas in our home was beautiful, but also a pain in the neck. Mother would stress out over all the preparation. All the kids were expected to do extra chores, bring boxes down from the attic, keep the tree from drying out, try to figure out why strings of lights wouldn't work, pretend to like fruitcake, etc. (Most Jews by birth don't know how lucky they are to avoid it all.)

I recall when I reached 16, my father led our family away from the Mormon faith because he no longer believed its tenets. Through my college years and the beginnings of my career, I led a secular, upwardly mobile life in Southern California. If anyone asked my religion I answered, "I am religiously anti-religious." Then, I fell in love with a woman who was raised at a Reform temple in Los Angeles.

I wanted to ask her to marry me, but I was afraid that her response would be, "I can't marry you because you're not Jewish." To get around that potential roadblock I schemed that the best defense would be a good offense. I suggested we take an Introduction to Judaism class. I anticipated that we would go to class together and in the car on the way home I would state my case logically. I would get her to see that Judaism, or any religion, was not something we needed as we embarked on life together.

Class after class, I waited for the rabbi to say anything that I could expose. Instead, the classes kindled my soul. I decided that Judaism was something that I wanted for my family and me.

I became fully committed to my future wife in every way. Her family made me feel as welcome as a full member and I became involved with the Jewish community in my career and other ways. Her family became my family and her people became my people. If I had been more familiar with the Book of Ruth, it would have come as no surprise that inevitably her God would become my God.

After my conversion, my father jokingly said, "So out of the frying pan and into the fire." The "fire" must have been Judaism. I must declare that living life joyously as a Jew has been the fire that has warmed my life for the past 25 years.

When I discuss my conversion with Jews by birth, they usually ask two questions: "Was it hard to give up Jesus and Christmas?" and "What did your parents and family think?"

Many people assume that changing "tribes" can be a spiritual struggle and a strain on relationships. Many Jews by choice do go through the conflicts portrayed in movie and television plots, when couples intermarry or face cultural differences. However, my experience was rather seamless and without conflict. In fact, my path to conversion was like a soul returning to where it always belonged.

My family and friends had no difficulty about my becoming a Jew by choice. My extended non-Jewish family enjoys my immediate family *simchot*, such as events at my children's Jewish day school and their *bar/bat mitzvahs*. I know they love me no less because of my decision to become part of the Jewish community.

Roy Chesnut

I WAS BAPTIZED in the Union Congregational Church, which was so secular that members were not required to believe in Jesus Christ as the Messiah. My paternal grandmother's ancestors were pilgrims who came to America in the 1620s to escape religious persecution. Union Congregationalism started in America during colonial times in order to establish a township under English law. My grandmother was a college graduate and involved in the League of Women Voters.

We moved to California when I was 6 years old. My father was a physicist and, for him, science replaced religion. I recall hearing a story about how Jesus had brought a dead man back to life. I asked my father about it and he told me he didn't believe it. After that I didn't believe it either. A few weeks later, I also found out that Santa Claus was not real. In a strange way these two revelations are connected.

I was raised to think that all religions were equally valid, or should I say invalid, but it was OK for other people to believe in these things.

My father had a Jewish friend who went to graduate school with him and I became aware that his family was different when my mother said something about them not celebrating Christmas.

As a college freshman, I had my first friendship with a Jew. His name was Todd. Although a paraplegic, he wrote chapters for college-level chemistry textbooks, served on the board of the National Science Foundation and has had a very successful career as a drug researcher.

At UCLA, I met Jews with hats and beards, Jews with *yarmulkes*, Jews without *yarmulkes*, Jews with dark curly hair and brown eyes, and Jews with blond hair and blue eyes. I had no stereotype, no negative stigma.

After graduating from UCLA, I fell in love with a Jewish girl and we married 18 months later. I had no interest in converting at the time, but I wanted to be sure that my children knew Jewish culture. I felt that Judaism had a lot to offer and I wanted my children to benefit.

Nadine and I shopped around and found a Reform temple. I found services very deep and occasionally transforming. *Shabbat* morning services usually had a very stimulating discussion of the Torah portion and how its principles apply to life. These were usually really cool discussions with the rabbi and congregants.

The experience led me to think that it was time for me to convert since I thought of myself as Jewish. Actually, there were a few mind-blowing epiphanies that were followed by a lot of powerful dreams. It was all very mystical.

My remarkable rabbi sponsored my lengthy and challenging conversion. Life interfered. I had some health issues and a job change that slowed the process. Also, we were raising three children. And my wife was practicing law part time. We were too busy.

Eventually, I was ready for my *beit din* and a date was set. The date was September 12, 2001–the day after 9/11. How do you like that coincidence?

Today, my wife and I are deeply involved at our temple. My wife is the *havurah* coordinator and has successfully helped form several *havurot*. I go to services and enjoy the Torah portion. I read from the Torah several times a year. I also play the bass violin in the temple's *klezmer* band.

Rabbi John Crites-Borak

I NEVER EXPECTED to become a Jew. In fact, I gave up on religion completely after investigating many Christian faiths that ranged from mainstream traditional congregations to radical fundamentalist groups that spoke in tongues: Catholic, Baptist, Lutheran, Episcopalian, Presbyterian, Christian and Missionary Alliance, Christian Science, Pentecostal Four-Square and others. My soul did not feel at home in any of them.

Buddhism and meditation left me relaxed, but unfulfilled. For more than a year, I made occasional trips to attend services of the Native American Church on the Navajo Reservation in New Mexico's Four Corners area. The long nights of sitting in tepees around the fire, praying and chanting, and taking peyote were interesting, but not compelling.

For two years, I attended *est*, a kind of secular new-age religion of the mind in which the intellect rules all. Its promise to "transform" me left me more effective in the business world, but aching for something to nourish my soul. One evening during a seminar, I simply walked out the door and never looked back. No religion—not even a secular one—suited me. I would be merely spiritual and that would be enough.

And it was enough for many years. One night while listening to a radio talk show centering on religious issues, a caller asked the very questions I had pondered for some time: Why be religious? Isn't it enough to be spiritual? The talk show host thought for a moment and then replied: "Because religion is to spirituality as language is to thinking. It gives us a way to organize, develop and express what goes on in our souls just as language allows us to organize, develop and express what goes on in our minds."

I began to think about religion in a new way. My soul felt most at home in the Catholic Church. I loved the rituals of the Mass. Perhaps if I prayed and studied enough, I would come to believe in Jesus as the Christ. Meanwhile, at least my spiritual needs might be met.

It was difficult. I loved the Mass, but I could not accept its context. More than once I found myself arguing theology with the priest, trying to stretch belief across a wide gulf of reason. "It's simply a matter of faith," the priest explained in answer to most of my questions as I silently recalled Ayn Rand's definition of faith as the shortcut to false knowledge. "How does one get faith?" I once asked. "You pray," he replied. "I pray, Father," I said, "but all I get are questions." He told me to pray harder. I did. I got harder questions.

One Sunday morning, we argued again. He was furious. My questions were heretical. His answers depended on blind faith. We could not bridge the gap. A friend suggested that Judaism – a religion about which I had almost no knowledge – might be a better fit for me. Everything I knew about Jews could be stated in three short phrases: They wear odd little hats, they don't believe in Jesus and they don't eat pork.

I called five local synagogues at random and only one rabbi returned my call. He listened to my story. "John," he said when I finished, "I have bad news for you. We don't have the answer. Don't get me wrong, we have answers. We have more answers than you can count, but we don't have 'The Answer.' On the other hand," he continued, "if you are looking for a place where you can ask life's most profound questions and be willing to hear whatever comes back, then study a little, think things over, talk with others and have that be a way of life. Then, maybe you'd find a home with us."

He recommended the Introduction to Judaism course at what is now American Jewish University. I began the course with no intention to convert. After all, I had tried so many other things. Yet the more I learned, the more I found myself amazed at how good a fit Judaism was for me. It spoke to my head and my heart. It even felt right in my gut. Before the course ended, I came to believe that I had always been a Jew who never knew the truth. Although I appeared before the *beit din* and immersed in the *mikvah*, I have never felt that I converted to Judaism. I simply came home.

Two years later, I was eating dinner with Rabbi Debra Orenstein. "What are you going to do with your Judaism?" she asked. The question seemed odd to me. "What do you have in mind?" I asked. She paused for a long moment. "I was thinking you might want to become a rabbi." Converts can become rabbis? She assured me that they could.

As it happened, the *parashah* for that week was *Re'eh*. It begins, "*Re'eh anochi notein lifneichem ha-yom brachah u-klalah*"–"Behold, I set before you this day a blessing and a curse" (Deuteronomy 11:26). I had been working for a decade in public relations, at which I was good but not happy. The money was fine, but I went to sleep every night feeling vaguely unclean. Was God placing a choice before me, a blessing or a curse, the rabbinate or the status quo?

I imagined myself at the end of my life. I stood on the edge of my grave looking back over the days of my life. How did I want to say I used the precious and all-too-fleeting gift of life? Did I want my epitaph to read that I had sold some products, gotten some people elected and some ballot measures passed (many of which I personally would not vote for), or that I had done what I could to help people connect to the most effective, loving and nurturing way to live that I had ever even imagined? Put in those terms, the answer was easy.

I began rabbinical school at the age of 43. Four years and 12 semesters later, I became ordained a Conservative rabbi at the Ziegler School of Rabbinic Studies.

Like the Israelites of our Torah, I spent 40 years wandering through life before I found the Promised Land. It was a long and arduous journey. More than once I wanted to give up on living, but I'm glad I didn't. To know one's purpose in life is a rare gift and a blessing beyond measure. May we all discover the path God sets out for us and may we follow it with love, strength and courage.

According to Rabbi Ashi, although converts may not have been present at Sinai, their constellations were. God said, 'I make this covenant . . . with him that stands here this day . . . and also with him that is not here.'

Deuteronomy 29:14

Shehecheyanu:
The Response of the Beit Din

We accept you with love.
Not to supplant our depletion as a people
    nor to multiply our diminished numbers.
Not to compensate for Holocaust losses
    nor gain another member in our world congregation.

We accept you
    out of respect for your earnest study,
    your resolute conviction,
    the decision of your own free will.

It is an honor to bring you under the wings of the *Sh'chinah*.
With reverence and joy we add your new Hebrew name
    into the names of our community.

Blessed are you who enter the covenant of Torah
    and the practice of good deeds.
Blessed are You, Creator of humanity,
    who has enabled us to witness this sacred moment
    in your life and in ours and in the life of God.

Baruch Atah Adonai Eloheinu melech olam
Shehecheyanu v' kiy'manu v'higiyanu lazman hazeh.

Rabbi Harold M. Schulweis

M Y MOTHER GREW UP in an affluent black family in Arkansas. She was supposed to bring home someone with money, maybe a nice, black doctor. Instead, she insisted on Daddy, a Jew from Michigan.

He never participated in organized religion, but converted to Judaism at the insistence of his first wife. He figured it wasn't much of a stretch. The father he'd barely known was the son of a rabbi.

After that marriage failed, Daddy met my mother in Chicago. Shortly after their wedding, my sister and I arrived. By then, Daddy was an atheist. My mother was brought up in the African Methodist Episcopal Church, but ceased practicing after discovering New Age mysticism and spirituality. They compromised by ignoring religion entirely. When my sister and I were old enough, they reasoned, we could choose for ourselves.

I wasn't actively exploring when external forces put me on the path to Judaism. I'd become indignant about some blatant anti-Semitism I encountered in college. Even though I wasn't raised Jewish, I had Jewish ancestry and couldn't abide such things. I started studying Judaism, at first so I could argue more effectively with bigots. But the more I learned, the more it felt like a good fit for me. I converted soon after graduating from college.

I don't even think I was school age when I made up my mind to adopt. My father's horror stories about his experience with foster care moved me deeply. Plus, in the eyes of a child, there is nothing more horrific to imagine than growing up without parents. It struck me as a grave injustice. And earnest liberal that I was, I felt personally responsible for addressing that.

Apparently, the horse that Prince Charming was riding died en route. So with my 30s vanishing at an alarming rate, I decided to implement

Plan B. I received a foster-care license and adopted two of the six children I fostered through the years. My daughter, Kenya, is 5 years old and attends religious school. My son, Jacob, turned 3 in February.

I wasn't sure how raising black children Jewish would go over with social workers, so I took all my Judaica down whenever case workers made home visits. I wouldn't lie about my faith if asked directly, but I didn't feel the need to advertise it. I'd like to think it wouldn't have mattered, but I'm glad it was too late to do much about it.

I'm holding out for a black, Jewish millionaire who likes kids, but Sammy Davis Jr. is dead, Walter Mosley's married and Lenny Kravitz is, well, weird.

W HENEVER PEOPLE I KNOW are asked about a circumstance of their childhood that others consider unusual ("What was it like growing up as a twin? With gay parents? On a *kibbutz*?"), they are always a bit confused: With no other childhood to compare it to, theirs seemed no more notable than anyone else. So when people ask me what it was like growing up with a non-Jewish father and what it meant when, 20 years after I met him, he converted, I can only say that it felt exactly like I imagined childhood should be.

When my mom met my dad, the ex-Jesuit son of an apricot farmer, I was 4 years old and much more concerned with our preschool's hamster than with my mom's romantic life. John gave me rides on his shoulders and his sister had a swimming pool, so as far as I was concerned, he was perfect. He married my mom and, five years later, I joined them at the courthouse, where a judge asked me if I understood that the man who married my mother wanted to adopt me. I said yes, and just like that he was my dad.

By the time he met us, my dad's life included very few remnants of his rigorous Catholic past. He still had a great love for early liturgical music, a deep understanding of theology and philosophy (which would later guide his path toward conversion), and a handful of lingering habits. Hearing him say grace at a family Christmas meal, I once declared that he was "praying to the wrong God!" Still, I never felt my dad gave anything up for us. He had left Catholicism several years before he met my mom and has seldom, if ever, looked back.

His family may never quite accept my dad's departure from Catholicism, but they are curious about his new Jewish life and make thoughtful, if sometimes misguided, gestures toward my mom and me. His mother, who is now 102, sends me very religious Christmas cards but scratches out "Merry Christmas" and writes instead, "Happy Hanukkah." I don't have the heart to tell her that they print Hanukkah cards and, truthfully, I like hers better.

In his search for a new spiritual and theological direction, my dad approached Judaism as he does all other endeavors, from scuba diving to ham radio operation—methodically and passionately. He read everything he could get his hands on, taught himself biblical Hebrew—at one point, he even tried his hand at Rashi script—and kept up a rigorous correspondence with several rabbis. As he learned, so did I—not just about the subject matter he was poring over, but also about this man who had become my father.

Not having grown up in a Jewish environment, however, my dad also had a lot to learn about Judaism as a way of life. Had my mom been any less committed to her faith, he would have been content with Judaism as an intellectual pursuit and I would have grown up counting down the days until I didn't have to go to Sunday school anymore. Instead, she involved us both in the practices of Judaism she thought most important. We all had our pre-*Shabbat* tasks, rituals in their own right (hers: cooking; mine: polishing the candlesticks; my dad's: gathering together our photocopied prayer sheets). Her *Pesach Seders* took days to prepare and our guests lounged around the floor-level *Seder* table on piles of cushions and pillows. My mom's own relationship to Judaism is private and mysterious, even to me—but she has a deep and spiritual commitment to her faith and it is undoubtedly because of her that both my father and I are Jewish today.

They say that it takes a village, and many people outside our nuclear family helped nurture my Jewish identity. I spent the best summers of my young life at Camp Swig in Santa Rosa, California, and will forevermore advocate Jewish camping as a critical piece of bringing young people to Judaism. Once every summer, we would wake up before sunrise and hike up to a nearby plateau to watch the sun coming up over the trees. This was how I learned the *Shehecheyanu*, and it's the image I have in mind every time I've said it since. Later, I became a leader (eventually on the regional level) in the North American Federation for Temple Youth and at Washington University in St. Louis, Missouri. Looking back, almost every major landmark of my youth–from my first kiss to the funeral of a young friend–took place in a Jewish context.

As I learned more about Judaism at camp, in high school and during my Confirmation trip to Israel, I enthusiastically shared my knowledge and enthusiasm with my parents. And so it was that my strong Jewish identity also informed theirs. Seeing how important Jewish life was to me, my parents became more involved at our synagogue: taking classes, going on retreats and volunteering at the synagogue-operated food pantry.

By the time my dad finally converted, almost five years ago, most people who knew him considered his conversion a mere formality. To me, however, his becoming a Jew affected me in an admittedly unexpected way. Standing with my mom outside the *mikvah*, listening as he bobbed up and down while my childhood rabbi recited the blessings, I was proud not only of my dad, but also of my religion and my congregation for welcoming him so warmly. Most unexpectedly, I was proud of myself; of playing a part in my dad's journey to Judaism and, in so doing, enriching not only his life, but also my family and the Jewish community.

Being the child of what people call a "Jew by choice" has taught me that Judaism isn't simply something that is thrust upon you, but something that you work toward and that we who embrace Judaism are all Jews by choice.

I am now 25 and living in Washington, D.C., 3,000 miles from home. These days, my Jewish involvement is sporadic and informal, but still meaningful. I go to services at a few synagogues around town, mostly when there is a specific occasion–a holiday or *yahrzeit*–and attend events with the "young professional" groups run by the bigger synagogues. Like nearly all my Jewish friends, I date mostly Jewish men and have become good at explaining to non-Jewish prospects why a Jewish partner is important to me. I tell them (and myself) that the most fundamental things about who I am come from the experiences I had growing up in the Jewish community–at home, at camp, in Israel, even at Sunday school. I can't possibly make a life with someone to whom these things are foreign. But I often wonder how much of this "policy" is just what I think I should be doing and I am haunted by the question: What if my mom had dated only Jewish men?

My mom likes to say that the best Jews aren't always the ones you find; sometimes they're the ones that you make. Still, it takes a pretty remarkable person to do what my dad has done for himself and for our family. Perhaps the question is not whether or not someone has grown up Jewish – plenty of people who did aren't interested in living Jewish lives – or whether or not he or she would be *willing* to convert. More important, as my dad has taught me, is the question of whether or not someone can understand and appreciate the essence of Judaism, and its importance in my life.

As my father prepared to join the Jewish faith (and, literally, enter the land of Israel), he recited these last lines of the *Ve'ahavtah*, God's instructions to the wandering tribe of Hebrews as they prepared to enter the land of Israel and, in so doing, become the Jewish people, "Take to heart these instructions with which I command you this day, and teach them to your children" (Deuteronomy 6:6–7). My dad has honored this commandment above all others, taking Judaism into his heart and teaching me that being Jewish is both a challenge and a blessing, neither to be taken lightly. My humble prayer is that I can someday bless my own children in the same way.

Reprinted with permission of Reform Judaism magazine, published by the Union for Reform Judaism

Gail Freidman

MY EPISCOPAL/ANGLICAN FATHER and my Catholic mother did not choose a tradition in which to raise me. My father passed away when I was 7, and then my mother when I was 10. I was on my own and went to whatever place of worship my family or friends took me and where I saw similarities between religions.

Before my mother passed away, she told me I needed to find my own path in life and that I needed to go to California.

Consistently, I was attracted to workmates, girlfriends and dates who turned out to be Jewish. I celebrated Passover and Hanukkah with my friends and their families who took me in. I remember one Hanukkah with my childhood friend, Jill. Her aunt talked to me about my cartooning and encouraged me. No one did this for me. As an orphan, in a family that had known difficulties, I felt as if everyone waited for me to make a wrong move. Jill's aunt made me feel that I had potential. Wow! I wanted to adopt her. I loved my first feminist *Seder* with my friend Blair's mom during spring break. We had to go out and find more *matzo*. That was not so easy to do in 1982 in Raleigh, North Carolina. But we had a blast reading and singing until late into the night.

I played guitar with the Catholics, sang with the Anglicans in Canada during summers there with my father's parents, and celebrated holidays with Jewish friends. I felt a direct connection with God in Judaism that I could not satisfy in those other traditions. I really tried. I taught Sunday school for Catholic kindergarteners and focused on God's love.

During college, I served as my sorority's chaplain. The quotes I chose that rang true for me had to do with Father Abraham, Noah, and Jonah and the whale. I graduated college and began studying with a rabbi in Northern Virginia. After I moved to California, I took an Introduction to Judaism class at a Reform temple. I was stunned to find that the rabbi thought like me. No one thought like me!

My path was very quietly calling me. When I applied to graduate schools, I selected a few in California but was rejected. For a diversion, I took a trip to Spain for a conversational Spanish course with Northern Virginia Community College. I made fast friends with a classmate and we toured Jewish areas.

After my return to the U.S., the University of Southern California business school's admissions office called and informed me that I was denied in error.

The summer between my first and second years of graduate school, my grandmother asked me to visit her in Connecticut. On the return trip, I sat next to Jon, the man who would become my husband.

After I converted and after marriage, I studied for my *bat mitzvah*. Since then I've had two beautiful boys. What I've always wanted for myself, I have given to my children. They have parents and a family that love them very much and take interest in them. I now serve on the board of directors of the Jewish Community Center, sing and act in my temple's Purim show, and am a student in the Hadassah Leadership Academy. My husband studies Hebrew and is having his adult *bar mitzvah*. My son Joe studies Hebrew and is preparing for his *bar mitzvah* and my son Ben is beginning his formal religious education. All of this as a result of following my unlikely path.

Cheryl Gillies

OR A LONG TIME, my family and I had little religious tradition. We celebrated Christian holidays without believing what lay behind them and sang Christmas songs without thinking about the words. It was fun for the children until they grew older, and then the magic of Christmas faded and the holidays became presents and decorations that did not bring true happiness. I studied basic Christian texts and discussed the possibility of attending church with my husband, but he was not interested. Each passing year, we celebrated holidays in a secular way that left me with an increasing sense of dishonesty.

In search of a tradition that held some meaning and truth for me, I enrolled in a world religion class where I learned about Judaism and it intrigued me. Then I saw a full-page ad announcing a *Keruv* outreach program at Valley Beth Shalom. I attended all but one lecture that year.

My life could have continued the way it was, but my yearning led me on a journey that began with the selfish goal of finding a religion I could compartmentalize and bring me a sense of inner peace and purpose. Unconsciously, I chose a tradition that gave me much more. I fell in love with Judaism when I learned about *echad, tikkun olam*, and *shutafim*. The idea that God is one and connected to this world, that I am connected to God, was created *b'tselem Eloheim* and am in this world to contribute something unique to its repair was very exciting. *Tikkun olam* gives me a sense of purpose and a responsibility that is clear, uplifting and life-affirming. I gain a sense of purpose by acts of *tzedakah* that speak to my heart. Once I learned that I am *shutafim*—partners with God—that I witness God by feeding the hungry and clothing the naked, it became impossible to ignore. Judaism places emphasis on the deeds and actions one performs in this world, and the accountability of each person in this world hit home.

Born in Mexico to American parents of Swedish, Norwegian, Scottish, Russian and German backgrounds, I grew up in Central America and Kenya, and went to university in Europe. This eclectic mix is the reason I chose to become a Jew.

While in college in Warsaw, Poland, I visited Auschwitz. I was overwhelmed by the realization that if I had lived in Europe during the war, I would have been sent there or somewhere like Auschwitz because, despite my blond hair, blue eyes and Nordic features, my mother's father was Jewish. She never lived with him and was not brought up as a Jew, but that would not have mattered to the Germans.

I became engaged to a wonderful man who happened to be Jewish. Although his mother cared deeply that I was not Jewish, he didn't mind and had no plans to raise our children as Jews. But I felt differently. Having lived in so many places with so many different types of people, I believe that all religions are essentially the same at heart. The Ten Commandments or their equivalent are at the core of all faiths. Additionally, I had the chance to see some of the most beautiful places in the world and to know so many different people. I know there must be a divine hand in the world's creation and in the world's people. Therefore, I wanted to raise my children with a religious background.

I also know that people can be barbaric and if they want to hate you, they will find a reason to do so. I wanted my children to be raised as Jews because with a Jewish father, they would forever be identified as Jews. I believe you have to shout out who you are at the top of your lungs and I would not send my children out into the world unprepared. Consequently, after we were married, I decided to convert and have been a Jew by choice for 30 years.

My choice had more to do with issues of sociology than religion, but I found that the conversion process gave me a deep appreciation of Judaism.

I studied at the Jewish Theological Seminary in New York and thoroughly enjoyed learning the philosophical basis for Judaism. I studied at my mother-in-law's kitchen table and learned Yiddish. My three children went to Hebrew day schools and I learned the songs, chants and basics of a Jewish education. I volunteered for many years at the Bureau of Jewish Education and I saw the deep yearning of Jews for continuity.

I have not always found it easy being Jewish. I have heard my share of anti-Semitic jokes and comments. Speakers are often surprised when I confront them because they don't think I look Jewish. I have also had my share of anti-*shiksa* comments from the other end. I have been in a room where two people would discuss the shame of someone's son or daughter marrying a non-Jew more times than I care to remember.

I feel extremely fortunate to have found my synagogue where warmth, humor and genuine good will exemplify what I looked for when I decided to convert.

Now, if only I could get my husband to attend *shul!*

ॐ

"*Even as we find that Abraham and Sarah became proselytes and were blessed, so shall all proselytes who pattern themselves after their conduct be blessed.*"

Sefer Ha-Aggadah

Chris Hardin

I LEFT HOME IN SEATTLE, Washington, to work as a musical director on a cruise ship, roaming the Caribbean where I lived carefree, played shows and partied–to the fullest! A guest entertainer joined the ship for its summer run to Alaska. Jennifer Rea was a beautiful woman with the voice of an angel and full of life. We started to spend our "off" time together as well as our working time and eventually began dating.

One day, she turned to me and said, "What do you want from this relationship?" I said I wanted to marry her. I don't think she had a clue that I had any thoughts along those lines. I can't remember how long it was after that day when she told me she wanted to convert to Judaism and I needed to be OK with that if we were going to spend the rest of our lives together.

I knew nothing about Judaism. I grew up in a family that didn't pay much attention to the differences between people. My parents were musicians, and their friends and colleagues came from every race and walk of life. There was no awareness we were any different other than the obvious difference in the color of our skin. I told Jennifer if that's what she wanted to do, I didn't have any problem with it.

Eventually we left the ship life and Jenn continued to learn about Judaism, attending synagogue services, classes and reading about Jewish life. She encouraged me to join her, but I didn't have any interest in making a change. I was happy with my life. My religious background consisted of going to church because my father was the choir director for Lutheran and Presbyterian churches, and not for spiritual reasons. I did learn about God and religion from church and believed in a higher power. I was taught about the importance of being a good person and fearing God from my attendance in Sunday school as well as at home.

Jennifer's connection with Judaism began long before she met me. Even though I was nominally Christian, I didn't feel connected with the religion. I listened to the pastor and read the writings, but it didn't grab me. When Jenn brought up the Jewish issue, I had no thoughts one way or the other about it. If she wanted to pursue her interest, I would encourage and support her as much as possible.

We married and Jennifer continued to read, met with different rabbis and followed her quest toward Judaism. My own spiritual needs arose when our daughter was born in 1992. I wanted to help her learn about God and I wasn't the one to teach her.

Jennifer met with a rabbi at a Reform temple. He told her, as other rabbis had, that she couldn't convert by herself: Both husband and wife needed to make the journey together. At the time, I didn't understand why, but I agreed to accompany her with no intention of converting.

The rabbi said that he would like to be our teacher. However, he felt we would get a more thorough understanding of what it is to be a Jew by attending the Introduction to Judaism class at what is now American Jewish University.

Near the beginning of the classes, I began to feel like this was where I belonged. Our instructor was excellent, but the most powerful teacher was a book, *Jewish Literacy* by Rabbi Joseph Telushkin. It's a "Reader's Digest version" of what it is to be an observant Jew. I was drawn into it with every fiber of my being.

One instance stands out to me during our studies. During Rosh Hashana services that year, I sat in the nosebleed section of the congregation watching the service when suddenly I became totally alert and aware of my surroundings and what transpired on the *bimah*. A movement of light, much like an out-of-focus camera lens, began circling around the center of my attention. This might sound a little weird, but I felt as if God was telling me, "Yes Chris, this is the right thing for you to do."

It was a phenomenal sensation as well as my biggest turning point. I studied hard and long, wanting to know everything I could in the short amount of time we had with this class and this wonderful teacher. It all culminated with a written test, a *beit din*—an oral test given by three rabbis —and the ritual of the *mikvah*. For the first time in my life, I felt I belonged to a spiritual community. I experienced a strong sense of being grounded.

My dad and four younger sisters had the same reaction about my conversion. They were behind me all the way. The only negative came from the one sister who is a very devout Evangelical Christian. She was upset because she thought that I was going to "burn in hell" since I didn't accept Jesus as my savior. Her pastor pointed out to her that there are many paths to God and that she and I are actually closer because we both are pursuing that same goal in our own way. I don't have any idea what my mom would say, may she rest in peace. I would like to think that she would be OK with it, as she always supported everything I did.

Our religious community has been wonderful to us. From the beginning, everybody welcomed us with open arms, opening their homes and families to us. One of our children is active in United Synagogue Youth and the other attends day school. We continue to learn about Torah and what it means to be an observant Jew.

Ten years ago, I converted to Judaism and with each passing year I find myself desiring more knowledge and more involvement. I learned much about being a good person and how my actions affect both my immediate family and others. I strive to raise my children to be observant and am planting the seeds of *tikkun olam* as well as *tzedakah* in each of them. If my wife and I do that, then we will have done our part in making the world a better place.

One last thought: Judaism is the best-kept secret in the world. It's not for everybody, but those who embrace it and strive to live their lives according to its laws and teachings discover that it makes the world a better place. I will be forever grateful to my wife for her persistence in seeking this path. Her drive helped me discover this wonderful way of life.

FTER A SERIOUS CHILDHOOD ILLNESS, I began thinking about life and death. Three or four years after I recuperated, when I was in the fourth grade, I had a very strong need to be a part of a religious community. I wanted to think about God, I wanted to talk to and listen to people who knew more than I did. I wanted to learn a deeper way to think about my life. My parents were secular Christians and did not attend church. So I did the best I could and went to Catholic and Protestant churches with school friends. I was 9 years old and decided to walk to a small Lutheran Church about three blocks from our home where I filled out a card with my name and address. My parents were mortified a few days later when a representative from the church came to our door asking if we would be interested in attending regular services each week.

I proceeded to be baptized, attended catechism classes, was confirmed, and became the president of the youth group several years in a row. Not only did I attend religious and public school, I studied voice privately. I worked for a Christian Science Church in order to earn extra money and had to sing a new song each Sunday morning for the congregation.

At a certain point, I felt that Christianity did not answer my questions about life and living. I continued to work for the Christian Science Church and other churches, but decided to leave the Lutheran Church and youth group. My parents tried to talk me out of it, but I stood my ground. Six months later, they stopped going to church themselves.

I went to the University of California, Santa Barbara, and then moved south to Los Angeles to continue my singing career. One Friday night, I attended synagogue services and was absolutely mesmerized by the *bar mitzvah* who spoke about plans for his life. Imagine, a boy of 13 talking about the ethics of his life, what was important to him and how to better the world. He sounded so responsible. Wow! I had never seen anything like this before.

My boyfriend at the time was a nonobservant Jew. The defining moment for me was the first *Pesach* I attended with him and his extended family at his uncle's home. The story of the Exodus stunned me. How this group of people made the journey from slavery to freedom still has relevance today. What a brilliant way to teach a valuable lesson. Make it a holiday. Do it every year.

From that moment on, I began to ask questions, and my boyfriend's mother supplied me with books about the remarkable qualities of the Jews on a cultural and social level. There was so much to learn. How exciting.

About this time, I went with a friend of mine to see the nine-hour film *Shoah*. I had to find out why Jews are singled out. I had to figure this out.

There was something about Judaism that pulled at me and I began attending *Shabbat* and holiday services wherever I happened to be. So logical. So spiritual. So organized. The deeper I went, the more I realized how much there was to learn. I had many questions on many different levels.

While all this was going on, I met my future husband and we began dating. Chris was not Jewish. Within six months, he asked me to marry him and I told him I wanted to convert to Judaism. We married and I took classes at what is now American Jewish University, talked to rabbis and found Jews who attended synagogues. It wasn't until I was pregnant with our first child that I felt an overwhelming urge to make the conversion. I couldn't wait any longer. Even though I felt my Jewish education wasn't good enough, it no longer mattered. The time had come.

We attended different synagogues and spoke to many rabbis. I studied at a Reform temple where the rabbi thought it would be a mistake to convert unless my husband and I did it together. We went to several others, making appointments with rabbis at most of them. Then one rabbi we met with told us: "I may be making a mistake by sending you to learn in a Conservative environment. But instead of taking classes from us, go to the [American Jewish University] and get an extensive education."

We enrolled in a series of classes that spanned seven months with three hours of intense study each week. My husband and I had a weekly date.

Chris said he would "support" me and go because he knew how important it was. He also told me he had no plans to convert. The funny thing is that after one month of classes, he said, "Judaism is the best–kept secret."

We completed the class and went to the *beit din* and the *mikvah* with our one-year-old daughter. It was such a deep and meaningful time in our lives. We had always been close, but this process of conversion made our lives and our relationship deeper and more wonderful. It has only been a positive choice in our lives.

ෂ

A would–be Jew by choice is neither persuaded nor dissuaded.

Talmud *Yebamot* 47b

Embracing the Jew by Choice

Our Sages taught
You who come of your own accord into our family of faith
Are dearer to God than all the assembly of Israelites
Who stood before Mount Sinai.

For had they not witnessed
The thunder, lightning, quaking mountains
And the sounding of trumpets,
They would not have accepted the Torah.

But you saw no opening of the heavens,
Heard no peals of thunder,
Felt no earth moving beneath your feet.

You came of your own will
To trust in God, To join our family,
One with our fate and purpose.
To bind the wounds of the afflicted
And raise up the fallen.

Can anyone be dearer to God than this choosing person?
Who has come to us knowing
The history of our oppression
The residual forms of harassment in our own time
The record of Inquisition and pogroms
Of concentration camps and crematoria.

Come to us without reservation.
We honor the courage of your heart
The compassion of your soul.
You who enrich our family
Are blessed.

Rabbi Harold M. Schulweis

I STOOD IN THE CORNER and watched my 11-year-old daughter emerge from the *mikvah* and recite the requisite blessing. My son, soon-to-become a *bar mitzvah*, would follow minutes later. This would complete my little family's commitment to becoming members of the Jewish people.

For three years, we attended services at a Reform temple where the kids attended religious school, prepared to become *bar* and *bat mitzvah* and I became an active participant in temple life. Our synagogue was a huge part of our lives and our temple community was our second family. For my son's *bar mitzvah* service more than 250 temple friends shared in our significant and joyous moment. That was easily one of the happiest days of my life.

In retrospect, it was nothing short of a miracle. Less than 10 years earlier, along with my then-husband and two small children, I moved to Los Angeles, California, from the Caribbean. I knew a great deal about various world religions, but knew relatively little about Judaism.

Within months of arriving in Los Angeles, I found that almost everyone in my circle was Jewish. Even if they never set foot in a synagogue or if they ate cheeseburgers, bacon and shrimp every day, they knew they were Jews. And that sense of self was at the core of their lives. I gathered every book on Jewish history that I could find and I immersed myself in them. Paul Johnson's *A History of the Jews* was particularly useful.

What I uncovered in my voluminous reading was the narrative of a remarkable people, a people whose journey through thousands of years of history resonated most powerfully with my own soul. Here were my people. Persecuted and hated for doing right and good and true. Thank you, God. For no longer am I alone in this world of darkness. For about two years I did nothing more about it. I was busy changing careers, getting divorced and moving forward with my life. But once I moved into a new home, I began celebrating Hanukkah and Passover with my children. My connections and relationships with Jews continued to grow and I let many of my new friends know that I intended to convert. There were raised eyebrows, but no one discouraged me or encouraged me.

I was returning to a park to fetch my son from a pickup game of flag football and encountered one of the fathers, who I learned was a rabbi.

A few weeks later, I sat in his office. He suggested during that very first meeting that I join the temple. Soon a new Friday afternoon routine was set. I would stop seeing clients at 2 p.m., pick the kids up from school and together we would make *Shabbos* before heading off to temple for services.

I completed the Introduction to Judaism course, scheduled a date at the *mikvah* at American Jewish University, and one wet September day became a member of the Jewish people.

I was home at last. I needed to be among people whose core purpose matched mine.

I became part of a remarkable resurgence of light that was spearheaded and fostered by our rabbi. For me, the synagogue is a center of light and spiritual renewal, a place where people can come to replenish their souls after the wear and tear of daily life has taken its toll.

Choosing to become a Jew at this time, the beginning of this new millennium, when so much planetary change is afoot can seem to be quite the irrational choice. We have to become new Jews, awakened Jews. This is why I have chosen to be here, to be part of a people transformed and alive, fully accomplishing our covenant with *Adonai*.

Coming home has filled my heart with great happiness, and given my children and me an enormous sense of belonging. At home, *Shabbat* is the center of our week and our lives pulse to the rhythm of the Jewish calendar. Outside of our home, our synagogue is the hub of our world, it is our "village," and fellow temple members are the "family" with whom we share our path.

As my Jewish journey continues, I look forward to joining hands with Jews of all denominations, from all parts of the world, as we come together to fulfill our covenant with God to light the way for a new earth.

MY EARLIEST YEARS at my home in Trinidad were filled with fear. Fear of German submarines. Fear that if the Germans reached Dakar, Senegal, in Africa, we would be within range of their bombers. Fear of what the Germans would do if they invaded, because Trinidad produced oil and was the only British territory making high-octane gasoline.

Near the end of the war, when my grandparents would take me to the movies, I waited outside of the theater until after the newsreels showing Jewish victims of the Holocaust were finished. I did not know what a Jew looked like except for those emaciated people in the films.

Sometime in my late teens, my mother told me that I had Jewish ancestry. Cordelia (or Cordella) Henriques, a Sephardic Jew from Jamaica, had a row with her father because she wanted to marry a Christian. As a result, she told her father that she would raise all her children as Christians. Cordelia's daughter, Marianne Bravo Ford, married a Spaniard and their daughter was my grandmother.

After moving to California, I met my second wife, an Ashkenazi Jew from Chicago, Illinois. She said she wanted more connection with things Jewish. I went to a service with her and suddenly felt at home.

As my circle of friends widened, I began more and more to hearken back to Cordelia Henriques. My feeling of Jewishness became stronger and stronger—so strong that when we went to Florida for my mother-in-law's funeral, this little incident took place.

It was an Orthodox service and we were one man short of a *minyan*. My brother-in-law jumped up and exclaimed, "We do not have a *minyan*, Bill's not Jewish." My wife's brother-in-law told him, "Shush, Bill doesn't know it."

One summer day as we rode in the car, I turned to my wife, Wilma, and told her I wanted to convert. She was both surprised and delighted. I spoke to our rabbi, who had just retired. He suggested I speak to our cantor, who immediately offered to sponsor me.

I took classes and after several sessions, the senior rabbi told me that he believed my conversion would be more like me coming home. I agreed. I already felt I was a Jew.

Wilma R. Hitchins

O NE DAY, BILL SAID TO ME, "I want to convert to Judaism." I was startled. Although I was raised Jewish, I had fallen away from religion for more than 46 years. True, I went to synagogue for Rosh Hashana and Yom Kippur and a very occasional Friday night service. Also, I had *Seders* with my family and friends. I was connected by heredity and emotion to all Jewish causes and even visited Israel once.

"Why?" I blurted out.

My husband smiled warmly: "Because I feel like a Jewish soul. And I think it will bring us even closer."

I signed up to take conversion classes with him and was fascinated.

I had never learned most of the stuff they were teaching him. One Jewish book led to us reading and sharing both religious texts and secular material.

We decided to become active in our temple because we felt that would make the whole experience more meaningful. We were welcomed with open arms and afterward continued to be even more active. What a great time we've been having.

When I first saw Bill in a *tallit*, I started to cry. I cried through most of the conversion and even choked up at spending Rosh Hashana and Yom Kippur in temple with him during his first time as a Jew.

We continue our studies together and even volunteered to become do-cents at the Skirball Cultural Center. What a kick that is.

There's only one problem. I say, "*Gut Shabbos,*" and he says, "*Shabbat shalom.*" I'll learn.

David Tramain Johnson

I AM AFRICAN-AMERICAN and part American Indian.

Immediately after my birth, I contracted spinal meningitis and developed speech impairment. I went to a predominantly black school in Los Angeles, California, and then transferred to a Christian school where students made fun of me because of my speech problem. I did not like living with my speech impairment so I set my mind to overcome it. I transferred to another school where they helped me with my verbal skills.

In high school, I joined a predominately black church where I became a counselor and was one step closer to becoming a deacon. My Bible studies continued until I enrolled at a university where I met Jewish students, and found myself in a rabbi's home where I stayed for about four hours as he and three Orthodox students studied with me to help answer my questions.

I went to Hillel even though I was no longer a student. This changed my life forever. I became a Jew for a brief moment. Members of the *minyan* treated me as if I was one of their own. When visitors came, I told them how the service was conducted and what they needed to do. This surprised one person because she knew I was not Jewish.

I decided to find out what I needed to do in order to be Jewish. I searched the Internet and found an Introduction to Judaism class. The rabbi suggested trying the class for one day. After that, I enrolled. I also was in the process of moving back home where I had to deal with my parents and brothers. At my synagogue, I met a few other people who had come into the Jewish faith and who had similar difficulties with their families.

Before my conversion, I needed to choose a Jewish name. I went to the library and found a Jewish dictionary of names. I chose Joseph Zelig-Liss Finkelstein to commemorate the lost Jews who did not have a voice, who did not have someone to be there for them in time of need. This deals with every Jew who ever lived, the present and the Jews who will be born in the future.

My dad tried to convince me about the Christian faith and I tried to explain why I chose to be Jewish, but he did not understand. However, when the time arrived, he stopped attacking me. My mother, on the other hand, said she was very happy I was converting.

A total of eleven rabbis and other Jews helped me along the way to become a Jew. I never thought I would have so many people with me through my conversion. I now have a heritage with the Jewish people.

Thank you! Thank you!

Elisabeth Kesten

I WAS BORN AND RAISED Protestant in Nuremberg, Germany. From my earliest childhood I was drawn to the Bible. An avid reader, I searched for books about the time of Jesus because I wanted to know more about him. That's when I discovered Jesus was a Jew and I became interested in Judaism. I was 12 when I found out what the Germans did to the Jews during World War II. My parents never told me about the Holocaust and no one in Germany talked about it. (My father and mother were children during that time and had no contact with Jews. Later I discovered that my grandmother's second husband was an officer at the Eastern Front, responsible for the management of a camp where about 350 Jews worked. They all perished and he died as well.)

After reading Shalom Asch's books and similar writings, I became determined to learn more about Judaism. At the age of 13, I made my way to the Jewish home for the aging where they had a small synagogue. A couple that had moved back from Israel managed the home and one of their sons became my Hebrew teacher, although I had no desire to become Jewish. At 14, I became confirmed in the Protestant Church. Everyone was impressed that I studied Hebrew and thought I wanted to become a minister: a university career in Germany where students learn Latin, Greek and Hebrew. However, I stopped going to church and started attending synagogue. The Jews in Nuremberg received me with warmth and friendship, especially when they realized I could read all the prayers in the *siddur*.

I wrote my parents a letter when I was 15, telling them that I planned on becoming a Jew and did not wish to discuss theology with anyone. (Besides being a doctor's assistant in a hospital, my father was also a deacon of the church.) A Protestant evangelical minister told me I would go to hell for rejecting Jesus. I asked him if all the Jews murdered by the Germans would go to hell. He said they would. And I said, then I'll be with them and that would be fine with me.

In response to my letter, my father informed me I couldn't convert as long as I wasn't able to support myself. I finished the Gymnasium (college prep school), received my bachelor's degree and began to teach. In my first year, I met with a rabbi in Stuttgart, Germany. I had an accident before my appearance before the *beit din* and couldn't come to Stuttgart. When I recovered, the rabbi died. It took another year to find another rabbi. This one invited me straight to the *beit din* without an interview.

After becoming a Jew and teaching for three years, I felt I decided to make *aliyah* and go to Israel. My mother was very unhappy and all my German acquaintances declared me insane.

I went to Kibbutz Shomer HaTsa'ir, where I met my future husband, an American. I learned more Hebrew and attended a teaching seminary in Israel where I studied to be a teacher. I visited my boyfriend in the kibbutz and after graduation, we married and moved to California.

We now have two children. My family in Germany doesn't understand my choice to convert. My brother has outright anti-Jewish feelings. My sister is a psychiatrist and thinks Freud is God, and that I am somewhat mentally deficient to need religion. My other sister doesn't mind. But my mother still curses all the books I read. Only my father appreciates that I am a practicing Jew.

I have become a regular Torah reader in my synagogue and have never regretted my decision for one second. I am extremely happy to serve as a Torah reader and occasionally as a *hazzan* on *Shabbat* or in the morning *minyan*. I have taught Torah to adults – an incredible experience – and I still read because there's so much to learn.

Bob Kip

I WAS BORN IN San Francisco, California, in an Episcopal hospital, educated in Catholic schools, married in a Lutheran Church and I will die a Jew.

The religious affiliation of the hospital resulted from geographic convenience. My mother's Irish Catholic upbringing determined which schools I should attend. The marriage resulting from the Lutheran wedding ended in divorce from my Lutheran bride after three years.

My decision to die a Jew results from three main factors: the influence of good persons who happen to be Jews, a study of Jewish history and practice, and my synagogue membership

I didn't give much thought to Jewish religious beliefs until my marriage to Hilary, who was raised in a culturally Jewish household. Her father ate only kosher food and the family attended High Holiday services annually. Hilary's father, Ken, of blessed memory, was a *mensch*. The love he had for his daughter extended to me. Ken invited me to join in the family *Pesach Seder* and High Holiday services at his *shul*.

At High Holiday services, I was moved by the central role the Torah plays in the service. The key image of the ritual is a book, not the beautiful representations of impossible human suffering I had been raised with. The optimism and human potential I infer from the Torah appeals to me.

The next time I confronted the contrast of my mother's faith and my wife's was at the funeral of the mother of a longtime friend of Hilary's. The deceased had been Roman Catholic, but the widower was Jewish. So the graveside services incorporated both faiths. A priest performed the Catholic liturgy for the dead, reminding mourners that the deceased was now with God and was better off than those left behind. I have never found much comfort in this liturgy. The rabbi celebrated the woman's life and repeated happy memories known to the family. The Jewish practice reminded me that my life had a purpose other than the ultimate demise we all face.

My next step toward Judaism started with a push from my kids who were diagnosed with autism. We'd attended a presentation by a doctoral student who proposed that adults with autism are more functional and better satisfied if they participate in a religious community. There was no question that the community would be Jewish.

We started asking around. One benefit of having autistic children is that you generally meet people who are committed to helping others. At the time, the only provider was Valley Beth Shalom's *Shaare Tikvah* program. After a year, we had found a home. Our children are accepted and treated just as kids. The congregation has the vision and resources to support this and other programs.

I continued to read many books on Jewish themes and feel empowered by the concept of *tikkun olam* and the *mitzvah* of optimism. I place a high priority in the need for peace. I am a Jew.

I completed the Introduction to Judaism program at what is now American Jewish University and joined in the Covenant of Abraham. I attend weekly Saturday services. We observe *Shabbat* in our way and eat kosher food.

I have been very lucky to find Judaism. My family accepted my choice. My mother said, "Go, be Jewish," and participated in our *Shabbat* and holiday celebrations. I look forward to many years of observance and participation.

By Phyllis Kraemer, his wife

H E WAS NOT RAISED in a Christian home. He did not marry a Jew who asked that he consider conversion. He did not, as a non-Jewish adult, find an interest in Judaism and pursue it to conversion. Instead, having always identified himself as a Jew, his interest in serious Jewish study and his commitment to Jewish observance began as a young man, away from home in the army, as he looked for something to occupy his free time. And there, with passing time and increasing knowledge, began a growing and painful awareness that the Jewishness he had always taken for granted could no longer be taken for granted at all. My husband's story is about his deep sense of loss for what he believed had always been, and the struggle, hurt, and effort which led to his redemption.

Paul was born of a Jewish father and a Methodist mother at a time when lineage was determined only matrilineally. He was raised in a home where religion played absolutely no part, but Paul sincerely believed he was Jewish. Like many of his friends, my husband never had a Jewish education or Bar Mitzvah. The family never attended any kind of religious service. But throughout his youth, he lived in a Jewish neighborhood, was involved with a group of strongly-identified Jewish friends, and was profoundly influenced in social justice and moral issues by inspirational Jewish teachers in the exceptional high school he attended.

I met Paul when I was just 13, and after a three-year hiatus, we started going steady when I was 16. From that time on we were together constantly, and when I was 18 and he 21, we became engaged. Unfortunately, he was drafted into the army several months before our wedding. For the next two years, the Korean War largely determined the events of his life. After basic training, Paul was sent to finance school at Fort Benjamin

Harrison in Indianapolis. During the week he was busy, but his weekends were free. There would be no partying without me. How could he spend his time? There was chapel on Shabbat, and classes in Judaism on Sunday mornings. Nothing better to do! And so it began—a lifetime of study that ended only with his death! What began as a casual time filler evolved into a genuine love.

In the early years of his growing but still limited knowledge, a dawning awareness and a nagging doubt about his own Jewish legitimacy inspired Paul to ask his mother to undergo a formal Jewish conversion. He mistakenly believed that her conversion would make him a Jew as well. My mother-in-law, herself long a part of a Jewish community of friends and in-laws, lovingly obliged. And for a while, Paul seemed content. My only competition for his free time were the unending series of classes and lectures he attended, and the hours of reading and studying he did to satisfy his unquenchable thirst for knowledge about everything Jewish.

Though I had no interest in studying myself, and even less interest in any type of Jewish ritual, he began to insist on a certain amount of observance. We joined a synagogue. When our children were young, we began attending Friday night services as a couple. He demanded that our children go to Hebrew School, not only through Bar and Bat Mitzvah, but until they completed Hebrew High School. He agreed to send them to summer camp, but only if they attended Camp Ramah. When they were teenagers, we moved from New Jersey to Florida. There—still against my gut feelings, but with the additional influence on my children of their Ramah summers—they all finally persuaded me to keep a kosher home. We began lighting Shabbat candles and having Shabbat dinners together for the first time. And though we belonged to a conservative congregation, Paul regularly attended the classes of a Rosh Yeshiva in Miami.

In the years between his army days and the move to Florida, as his knowledge of Judaism grew, Paul's discomfort and self-doubt about his own Jewish authenticity also grew. At first, apparently in denial, he insisted that he "must have been converted at birth," though his mother had no memory of it one way or the other. Then he went through a period in which he refused to address the subject at all. When our son David went first to Brandeis University and then to the Jewish Theological Seminary to major in Jewish studies, Paul could not have been more proud. Yet he seemed even more confused and more contentious about himself. Any discussion about his Jewish status made him angry. Those of us who knew and loved him could feel his inner pain.

During this same period, Paul and I were very involved with the Jewish Federation and the United Jewish Appeal. We were in Israel several times. Paul was very aware of the Right of Return and the power held by the Orthodox community there to determine who was a Jew. He knew that only an Orthodox conversion would be accepted in Israel and therefore he considered it "the most genuine." Though he never spoke to any of us about a conversion for himself, it became obvious that he was considering it when he finally spoke to the Rosh Yeshiva. Unfortunately, he was told that his conversion depended on my agreement to go the *mikvah* monthly. "No way!" was my answer. And so his conversion was put on hold.

After moving to Los Angeles, our daughter found an Orthodox rabbi who was more open. What a difference a rabbi can make! This lovely man made my husband feel totally accepted and valued. He listened to Paul's story, was amazed at the depth of his knowledge, and was delighted with the way we had raised our children. He was greatly impressed that David had chosen Jewish academia as a career. The only requirement he had of me was that I agree to another wedding ceremony—an Orthodox one. I loved the idea. The day Paul went to the *mikvah*, appeared before the Beit Din and was converted, will remain forever indelible in my mind. As I arrived to get him, Paul was standing in the middle of the street, dodging traffic. He was giggling with delight. His arms were raised to the sky in the World War II sign of victory. He was jubilant, the happiest man I had ever seen. Finally, after so many years, he was the Jew that he wanted to be. He could talk openly about his Jewishness and not worry about a challenge to its legitimacy. And we both loved standing under the *chuppah*, this time held by our children, as we again repeated our vows.

The legacy Paul left our entire family is remarkable. As their father wished, our three children married caring and exceptionally dedicated and practicing Jews. They provided Jewish day school educations for our grandchildren. Shabbat and Jewish holidays play important roles in all of their lives. All have been imbued with solid Jewish values and engrained with the idea of doing *mitzvot*. The entire family sees life and lives life through a Jewish lens.

After 56 years of being together and 53 years of marriage, my dearest husband died, but his legacy now includes me. I was the stubborn one, the rebel, the secular Jew who resisted everything religious. But to honor Paul's life and his memory, I became an adult Bat Mitzvah. Nothing would have pleased him more. And to my utter amazement, nothing has made me happier since his death than to involve myself in study and religious practice. During Shabbat services I feel him next to me, smiling. I continue to attend services on Shabbat. I think of my extraordinary husband every day of my life. Our children loved and admired him deeply. Our grandchildren adored being with him and remember him as the "kid who played with them and never grew old." On the occasion of his 75th birthday, David told Paul that he was his hero. But I consider myself the luckiest of all. He chose me and made my life so rich and meaningful. I am so proud to have been his wife.

ॐ

> *. . . since you have entered beneath the wings of the Divine Presence and attached yourself to Him, there is no difference between us and you . . .*

Maimonides, *Responsa* 42

WHEN PEOPLE DISCOVER I am Mexican and Jewish, they often ask if I was born Jewish or if I converted. While I know that they ask with good intentions and do not mean any harm, I tend to take offense at the question because I am not an inanimate, moldable object that can simply change from one form to another. I chose to embrace Judaism into my life.

I attended Catholic school during my primary school years. However, instead of making me grow closer to the faith, it actually pushed me away. I did not like the belief that if I sin I am going to be damned to hell unless I say a few Hail Marys and confess my sins to a priest. On the other hand, I could never question the priest about his sins and was put off when I questioned aspects of Catholic dogma. Finally, I had the impression that you are supposed to do well and repent your sins – not to make you a better person, but for the sole, and selfish, reason of getting into heaven. Since I did not believe in hell or agree with the "system," I began withdrawing from Catholicism.

Many people probably believe my exposure to Judaism happened because I had the good fortune to work at a synagogue. But it really began in Mexico, where we lived in a very exclusive area of Guadalajara heavily populated by Jewish families ranging from Reform to Orthodox and where many of my close friends were Jewish.

They introduced me to Judaism. When I saw them getting together with their families for weekly *Shabbat* dinners and holidays, I felt something was missing in my soul.

My hunger grew for a connection with a religion and a God that made sense. What I was looking for was right under my nose all the time. During my tenure at the synagogue, I found that what I searched for in religion occurred on a regular basis. As part of the service, the rabbi commented on the *Tanach* and the congregation could question and debate him.

On Yom Kippur, congregants confessed their sins and asked for forgiveness from both God and the one they sinned upon, but not to get into heaven. Rather, they did so in order to make themselves better and more complete individuals. Finally, I observed firsthand how Judaism embraced family and community through celebration of holidays and events throughout the year.

As a Jew by choice who struggled through many obstacles in pursuing my path to Judaism, I can't understand why so many of the younger generation of Jews intermarry and fail to keep the faith and traditions of Judaism alive and ongoing for generations to come.

M Y MOTHER LOOKS LIKE a conservative woman from Kansas, but in actuality is a "hard-core atheist peace activist." She and my dad divorced when I was 19. She remarried to a great guy. My father, a recovering Catholic, joined the Peace Corps at 55. I went to college in Chicago, Illinois, and headed out to Los Angeles, California, after graduation.

I was arrested while driving on LSD, and to avoid jail time I became sober. I still had all my problems because my drug of choice, alcohol, was taken away. Hollywood came to the rescue when the Screen Actors Guild gave me health insurance. My girlfriend at the time suggested I use it for therapy.

One of the first things my therapist asked me about was God. That threw me. Like any good atheist, I thought mental health and spirituality were two different things. He gave me the old "it takes as much faith to know there is no God as it does to know there is a God." This never fazed me before because my surefire checkmate answer was always, "Uh-uh!"

All of a sudden, my spiritual door cracked open to the idea of a spiritual path. This crack happened to coincide with my relationship with Jennifer. I wanted to marry her and it became apparent that I had to know a bit about Judaism to show that I respected her family's beliefs. Jennifer and her parents never made me feel I had to convert (OK, maybe her grandmother mentioned it a few dozen times). But they did go to synagogue on the High Holidays and lit candles on *Shabbat*. Passover was a huge deal. Jennifer and her sister had attended Hebrew school. I realized I needed to learn about Judaism since it was in my life and it would be a good idea to demonstrate my respect for her religion.

I took an Introduction to Judaism class. The curriculum was great, but instead I refer people to Rabbi Harold Schulweis' book, *For Those Who Can't Believe*. He explained why bad things happened to good people:

laws of nature and free will. It changed the way I looked at spirituality. I was still skeptical, but not as cynical. I was open to answers instead of dismissing them outright. Rabbi Schulweis sponsored me during my conversion and later officiated at Jennifer and my wedding.

I had never thought about actually converting, but I now knew I was headed down this interesting path. You know you are taking conversion seriously when you allow a strange man to circumcise you . . . again! How did I get here?

I read *The Jew in the Lotus* and loved it. It's about a group of rabbis invited to India to meet with the Dalai Lama. One of the rabbis was Jonathan Omer-Man, an English Jew confined to a wheelchair. Rabbi Omer-Man was interested in keeping Jews from leaving Judaism for Buddhism and helping them find what they were looking for in Judaism. Meditation combined with my Jewish reading provided the first real relief from my alcoholism and that's what brought me to my circumcision. As it can only happen in Los Angeles, my *mohel* told me his son was directing a movie and I was thinking he's pitching a stupid indie his son is making. Then I realized I knew his son and had auditioned for his film the day before, and now my *mohel* will put in a good word for me. I actually got a "call back" audition!

Now the deed was done, and there was no turning back. At the *beit din*, three rabbis gave me an oral exam. My rabbi was there, but the other two were hired guns from what is now American Jewish University. I got through it and went to the *mikvah* where I got naked, dunked three times and said three different blessings while two rabbis observed. They were sweet old guys and I really enjoyed it. The Jews know what they're doing. My cynical self analyzed if I had a spiritual experience.

So here I am. I have become everything I wasn't. I'm a sober, married, meditating, God-believing Jew. So do I believe in God? I do. I can't believe it, but I do. After I meditate every morning, I pray. And I laugh as I'm doing it because I believe this stuff. But I do.

Here's what I believe:

1. I am not God. That's the biggie. I may not know who He is, but I do know I'm not Him.

2. I believe that qualities such as compassion, love and surrender are not qualities that exist to feed and clothe us. And yet we all have them.

3. For me, God is a gerund. God is being godly–being loving, caring, humble and helpful. It is in the action.

Cantor Lorna Lembeck

I WAS 10 YEARS OLD the first time I openly professed a desire to become Jewish. I was exposed to Judaism through a school friend, because I sometimes tagged along with her to Hebrew school. It wasn't long before I was asking my mother if I too could be Jewish like my friend, go to Hebrew school and become a *bat mitzvah*. My mother's initial reaction was shock, followed by my immediate enrollment in a Sunday school program at a nearby church. I stopped attending after a short time, and also avoided going to synagogue events with my friend because I knew I would always be an outsider.

However, my early experience lit a spark that smoldered for many years until my life finally arranged itself in such a way that I could no longer deny the voice inside me. I knew I was supposed to have been born a Jew. After studying in the conversion program at what is now American Jewish University in Los Angeles, California, I stepped into the *mikvah* with my daughter and never looked back. The last 10 years of my life have been a tremendous journey of learning and transformation.

I chose Judaism somewhat late in life, but I believe that, subsequently, the cantorate chose me. Having had a previous career as a singer and actress greatly assisted in developing an ear for the magnificent musical liturgy I now studied. It wasn't long before I was asked to sing in the synagogue. Soon thereafter, I was a soloist in a choir. After that, I was asked to lead services.

I look forward to infusing members of a congregation with the passion I feel for Judaism through music, study, prayer and *simcha* as their cantor. I am totally invested in my spirit/voice connection. I sing with my heart and soul. I pray for and with my congregation. I want to engage worshippers in a meaningful experience, impact them in services and somehow inspire them to invite the traditions of Judaism into their lives as I did into mine.

Ultimately, we are all Jews by choice. We can choose out just as easily as we can choose in. This is not simply a new career path for me. It is a calling. It is a labor of love. When I teach a preschool child the *Shema*, or see the look of elation on a *bar/bat mitzvah* student's face when he or she has finally mastered a *Haftarah* or encourage a woman in her 80s who has never read from the Torah to study and become *bat mitzvah*, I know that I am where I am supposed to be.

I intend to impart the same enthusiasm and dedication to a congregation that has propelled me through this wonderful crucible of study and spiritual transformation, leading me to the next phase of an incredible journey. At a time of life when some people are slowing down, I feel that I am just revving up.

Baruch Atah Adonai Eloheinu melech olam
Shehecheyanu v' kiy'manu v'higiyanu lazman hazeh.

Michael Lembeck

I THINK IT WOULD BE FAIR to say that my life as a Jew and the practice of my chosen religion lay dormant for many, many years.

Lorna and I met when we were actors in an off-Broadway musical in New York, New York. We both came from secular families although her family was Episcopal. It wasn't as if Lorna and I weren't two people seeking spirituality, we subscribed strongly to an ethical lifestyle, believed in the importance of kindness, and were moved by the goodness and charity of others.

We married and became a blended family. I had a son and she had a young daughter. When Sam began his *bar mitzvah* tutoring a year before his big day, his *bar mitzvah* tutor came to the house once a week and spent quite a few hours with him. And I discovered Lorna sneaking into the room just about every week.

She had questions, she had thoughts and she was getting invested emotionally. And during this very important year, our daughter, who celebrated Hanukkah and Christmas, asked the big question, "Mom, am I Hanukkah or Christmas?" Our search for truth began.

On the morning of Sam's *bar mitzvah*, Lorna was percolating. This was the day she decided to seek out that which would enlighten her emptiness and show her a way–maybe the way–to a spiritual life she desperately wanted.

Lorna enrolled herself in the program and it wasn't long before she realized she wanted to convert, to become a Jew by choice. Moving quickly ahead, she converted and was not alone in the *mikvah*; her daughter Mimi also converted.

And thus was born the Lorna Lembeck who now realized, "I need so much more." She enrolled in the then-named Academy for Jewish Religion, not really having any idea where she was headed, or how she would use the education she was about to receive. She went on to get a master's degree in sacred music. Her future revealed itself to her during her studies. Lorna has perhaps the most beautiful voice any congregation will ever hear. When she began learning the musical liturgy, three things happened. One, she realized how much she loved singing the liturgy. Two, she made an intimate voice/spirit connection that was profound, soulful and moving. Three, she had an epiphany that the cantor gets to sing these magnificent prayers for a living. She learned as she became a cantorial soloist that she was having a profound and moving impact on congregations that heard her sing. She was encouraged to hurry up and learn as fast as she could so she could perform more services, get ordained and have a pulpit.

At her first High Holy Days for a congregation of about 1,000 worshippers, she transformed the congregants and gave them an emotional experience. I never experienced this myself when I went to synagogue as a youth and now I can.

Lorna leads *Shabbat* services twice a month, where I accompany her. She conducts Saturday morning services when the regular cantor is otherwise occupied. She teaches *B'nai Mitzvah* students and is beginning to do all kinds of life-cycle events.

Her transformed life has transformed my life and brought me back to Judaism with a passion I didn't think I was capable of having. My daughter is getting a master's degree at the American Jewish University and keeps kosher. My son is willing to attend any and all things Jewish, because he, like me, has returned to the fold and articulated how important it is for us to worship as a family. Lorna did this. She is doing it out there in the world as well. She is going to make Jews. She is going to make a difference.

Cheryl Lorenzo

I HAVE PARENTS who are Christians of differing faiths. As a result, we did not have a strong religious identity. That may have led to other challenges in their marriage, which lasted only 10 years.

As adults, my sisters became Seventh-day Adventists. They have similar practices to Judaism. Therefore, I was exposed to their practices and became used to their customs through the years. That made accepting Judaism a little easier for me.

I was first introduced to Judaism when my boyfriend suggested we take an Introduction to Judaism class together. He wanted me to feel comfortable around his family, and since the High Holy Days were coming up, this would help me feel comfortable by the time I accompanied him to the synagogue.

During the course of my study, many of the core beliefs really resonated within me. The importance of doing good in the world (*tikkun olam*), the high value placed on the role of women in both a biblical and contemporary setting, the belief in God as a higher power and not a human being elevated to that of a deity, the acceptance and warmth of Judaism and tolerance of all peoples. The Jewish conscience spoke to my heart. I was always a very spiritual person, but never felt a connection to any particular faith until now.

My family and close friends have been excited, supportive, positive and very curious. They want to understand what led me to this point and what I enjoy about the Jewish religion. They are curious about the religious practices and obligations that I have now undertaken and I take great pride in explaining what I have learned and how I participate in my new Jewish life.

My family feels it is wonderful for my fiancé and me to share our religious faith and beliefs. They also agree that it will build a solid foundation for our relationship and any children we may have. As our wedding approaches, I look forward to being married and starting our family. Should I be blessed with children, I want to share with them my journey and my spirituality.

Tree McCurdy

W HEN I WAS THIRTY-THREE YEARS OLD I had a nervous breakdown. Two, actually, within five months. This should not have been entirely unexpected, after spending my twenties struggling with disease, misdiagnosis, mistreatment, and depression. I'd thought that once the daily battle with pain and exhaustion was over, it would be like having wings. I would be able to redirect so much energy and willpower to finally accomplishing something with my life.

Instead, after my final surgery I felt chained to a roller coaster. My simple and happy job was eliminated, I recognized the love of my life, watched my chosen family disintegrate, we conceived despite precautions, but complications set in. My love was commuting to a poor-paying graveyard shift in a crime-ridden neighborhood; I could not get an job interview. We ran out of food twice, rescued by family and friends. There was a legal battle sucking away money we didn't have trying to find his daughter. Then came the drawn-out cancer scare. Instead of the health I'd fought for so long, there were months of botched paperwork, snippy phone calls, confusion with doctors, and finally a biopsy that might permanently affect my ability to ever carry children.

I'd never been a model of stability. I've been a model of stubbornness. The disease had started at twelve or fourteen hidden by the pain of changes I wasn't supposed to complain about. I'd always been was one of those profoundly alienated straight-A children, sensitive and trauma-prone, troubled at home and deeply troubled within. It's too easy to speak of "bad things that can happen," as if they were incidents that can rise up and block or even knock us off the beaten track. There is no beaten track growing up mentally ill. There is no "normal" to which to return.

At thirty-three, I knew I needed to head off a third breakdown. I was medically cleared to exercise again, determined to build myself up to

health, to sweat and pump and punish my body until it finally earned my
trust. I ended up on the polished wooden floor of that huge aerobics class
with the great mirrored wall front and center. The room filled up with
buff, tanned yuppies in coordinated exercise gear, moving with professional polish . . . and there I was gimping and swaying trying to keep up.
Baggy old t-shirt, baggy worn plaid pants, a kerchief wrapped around my
head to keep it covered and hide my thin hair. I looked so unutterably
ridiculous, like a frog in a clown costume. There was nothing I could do
but laugh at that poor, pitiful reflection in the mirror. I was too tired to
bear the humiliation of being me anymore, so I let it go. I let go of all the
promises I'd made to myself, all the expectations I'd demanded of myself
and failed. I forgave myself for being me. I forgave myself for getting sick,
and being broken, and not accomplishing anything with my life. There
was a sense of tremendous release as it all fell away, and then I was flooded
by a sense of unconditional love for the poor clown in the mirror.

Kol nidray, v'ehsoray, u'shvuay, va'chara-may . . . all vows, obligations,
oaths, anathemas . . . we do repent.

This is my Judaism. It is the Judaism of the Survivor. It is the Judaism
understood by Jeremiah and by the broken heart behind the Psalms. It is
the Judaism of despair, questioning, perseverance, and defiant celebration
through the Torah, the Middle Ages, and horrors of the Industrial Age.
It is not popular Judaism today. A charismatic rabbi recently wrote that
we need to lose the whole "survival" motif; it is too much of a downer and
irrelevant today and it's turning off the next generation.

But I understand the need to rage at the Almighty. I understand the
need to beat one's own breast. I understand the need to learn, and to keep
learning, all the time. I understand the need to see and celebrate each
precious blessing as it passes, to never let life shrink down smaller than a
hundred blessings a day. I understand that there is no normal, no Temple
to which to return, and there is no course of action provided by life as
trustworthy as a beaten track laid out within, carried within, the walk one
shapes one's life by. I have always cooked, cleaned, traveled, and sacrificed
for those I knew were in greater need than me. I have held the hands of
women in childbirth, and I have buried too many dead too soon. I have

watched the smallest insensitivity burgeon into the cruelest tragedies, and I do not understand what people mean when they say we are not living in the same world as our ancestors.

I've been rejected and challenged by Rabbis who feared I was seeking some sort of salvation or mystic rescue from Judaism. It isn't that. I just recognized the truth I already knew. They say the souls of the converts were brought to witness Sinai, then held in reserve and distributed through the ages to guarantee Judaism would always have a sense of fresh revelation, and adult wonder. I have been brought *m'mitzraim l'am yisrael*, out from the Narrow Place to the Nation of Israel. It's just taken me a while to catch up.

Dianne Nitzahn

I ALWAYS FELT A PROFOUND CONNECTION to God and desperately wanted to find a branch of Christianity that made sense to me. The turning point came when I was 17. I took a French class at a local community college. The instructor, David Forbes Pardess, was a Jew by choice and we became friends. He invited my fiancé, Michael, and me to his home for *Shabbat* dinner and other holidays. David was the first person I knew who answered every question and challenged me.

He taught me the Hebrew *Aleph-Bet*, basic vocabulary and blessings, and the *Shema*. The amazing feeling of peace and beauty that enveloped me that Friday night remains with me today.

I finally made the decision to join the Jewish community and enrolled in classes at what is now American Jewish University. I wanted to be Jewish, but how could I promise a *beit din* I would lead a Jewish life if I married a non-Jew? Michael took it seriously and I was astounded the day he announced he had gone to a *mohel* for a ritual circumcision a month before classes ended. We converted together and a few months later we chose a new last name that we felt was a perfect metaphor for our new life: *Nitzahn*, which means "bud" or "blossom" in Hebrew.

My father moved far away both geographically and emotionally. It never occurred to me that my family would have an opinion about my choice of religion or identity. My mother was upset until her minister told her that Christ was a Jew and if it was good enough for him, it was good enough for me. After that, she accepted our decision. She attended my adult *bat mitzvah*, and walked me down the aisle with my stepfather when Michael and I married at Valley Beth Shalom.

My oldest sister shares the same religious views as my father and my second sister felt I had separated from the family although we developed a good relationship later. My youngest sister could not fathom why I made such a drastic change in my life. However, we reconciled when she admitted she had been wrong to judge me and seemed impressed by my commitment to Judaism. Over time, my father has seen the positive influence of Judaism on our lives.

The Jewish community made up for my lack of family. The overwhelming majority have welcomed me and gone out of their way to make me feel accepted and comfortable. We have made Jewish friends outside the synagogue and I understand the warm kinship among Jews, even those would do not consider themselves religious.

Yiddishkayt develops slowly, but I feel I belong. Being Jewish has brought me a deep sense of happiness and fulfillment, and I am profoundly grateful to God for helping me find and embrace Judaism and the Jewish people.

ॐ

A Jew by choice is dearer to God than was Israel at Sinai, for he accepts heaven's yoke without having witnessed the thunders and trumpet blasts which attended the Revelation.

Tanhuma Lech Lecha 6

Juliana Boehnlein Olinka

I STARTED LIFE as a good Catholic girl in the suburbs of Detroit, Michigan, the first born of a family of 11 siblings. I attended parochial school for 12 years, went to Mass six days a week for the eight years of my elementary education, and at least once a week for the next four years of high school. At one time I even entertained thoughts of becoming a nun like most of the girls of my upbringing.

As far as I knew, everyone in my neighborhood was Christian, if not Catholic. But I remember my father's friend at work whom I learned later was Jewish. Our family dentist was also Jewish – but again, that wasn't an issue, as it wasn't a topic of conversation.

I moved away when I went to college, and began to widen my horizons. I met new people in the theatre department, where a Jewish graduate student became one of my dearest friends. But religion was never discussed.

In summer stock, I met my first husband – a non-Catholic farm boy. We married after my graduation, and moved to Atlanta to pursue our acting careers. I continued practicing my Catholicism despite choosing a mate from outside my religion. My marriage began to fall apart after less than a year. How could this happen? I prayed. No immediate answers were forthcoming.

We separated, and I moved back with my parents still hoping we could make it work. After all, I'd made a commitment and divorce wasn't an option in the Catholic Church. Unfortunately, marriage wasn't an option either. There wasn't anything to save.

I moved to New York City, alone. I prayed. I asked how to make it right. What had I done wrong? Where was God? No answer. The religion that was supposed to sustain and help me wasn't providing the support and sustenance I needed. I began to ask questions. Why confession? Why couldn't I go directly to God? Why did I have to confess to someone who stood between God and me? My Sunday Mass attendance became more sporadic.

With my career not yet flourishing, I started doing bookkeeping at an entertainment-related company where I met a wonderful woman. We became friends, and talked about life and love and Judaism. She told me in bits and pieces about herself. It resonated within me. Helen gave me a mezuzah and told me about the prayer inside. It meant a lot to me, and she did too.

Not long after, I met the Jewish man who would become my husband. We dated and fell in love. That's the short version. My church going had fallen completely by the wayside. The satisfaction, succor, support I should have felt from the religion of my childhood was missing. I couldn't practice it with the same sense of willing commitment.

The first High Holidays we were together, he went to services with his family. I stayed in the apartment and looked through his father's High Holiday mahzor. I read some of the prayers, and they were a revelation. I could ask for forgiveness directly–I didn't have to go confess to a priest. I attended my first Seder with his whole family. They were a delight, and Seder was amazing. We spent more and more time with his family and "Things Jewish" were becoming more and more interesting to me.

We moved to California so my fiancé could pursue his writing career, and decided to marry. But we talked about religion and children. If we were to have children, I was committed to the idea that they would have only one religion. My husband had a true New York Jew's appreciation of Jewish culture (although observance may not be high on his list) and he would always remain Jewish, so that left one choice: Join him. I signed up for an Introduction to Judaism class at Hebrew Union College, but we both attended. We were in the middle of the course when we decided to get married.

I passed the class with flying colors, and formally accepted Judaism in April, 1980. With a year's free membership at the temple, I joined the Sisterhood, took Hebrew language classes, hosted our own Seders for friends, and our Jewish life began together. Soon, we began attending a

Conservative synagogue for High Holiday services and sometimes on Friday evening.

In 1984, I became pregnant, and faced a conundrum: I'd converted in the Reform tradition but wanted my son to be accepted in Israel, and I feared we weren't as kosher as we needed to be. I decided to convert in the Conservative tradition. I went before a *beit din*, attended the *mikvah* at what is now the American Jewish University, and finally felt my conversion was indeed "kosher." After our son's birth, we eventually found a pre-school and Kindergarten at a Jewish community center, where we learned about a Conservative synagogue offering a free year of Hebrew School to new members. That became our new home.

When I learned that an adult *b'nai mitzvah* class was forming, there was no question! I needed to become a *bat mitzvah*. My son would go through the same experience before long and I needed to know even more about being a Jew. My *bat mitzvah* was a joyous celebration. I'll never forget standing on the *bimah* and chanting my parshah it for the first time. The *gabbai* was so proud of us. His smile gave me the courage and encouragement to sing my best to God.

Initially, my family did not accept the choices I made–in marriage or religion. But I was lucky to celebrate 26 years of marriage before my husband passed away recently, and now, over 26 years of choosing Judaism. I'm on good terms with my parents, who've "come around." My brothers and sisters and I are all connected, and always will be.

Being Jewish means so much to me. It's my connection to ethics and prayer, education and educating, friends and family, and to making the world a better place. It guides my choices. It is who I am. I got here because of the choices I made throughout my life, and I wouldn't change a thing.

David Forbes Pardess

My father would have told you he was a Southern Baptist and my mother, who was "spiritual but not religious," would have said she didn't believe any of it. They moved to Southern California from Oklahoma in the early 1940s to work in the Long Beach shipyards. We lived in San Pedro, California, and had big family Easter dinners and beautiful, exciting Christmases. I went to Sunday schools where I received a good sampling of Protestant teachings and attitudes. On the other hand, I warmed to the quiet, beautiful and mystical Episcopal and Catholic churches. People who attended them seemed religious in a real, earthy way. I used to go to mass with my mother's friend and wanted to be Catholic. Because of anti-Catholic sentiments in my family, I was baptized and confirmed in the Episcopal Church.

The only Jews I knew of appeared on television and in the movies. I remember an old movie where a rabbi and cantor conducted some kind of service. The Hebrew language, music and their ceremonial attire struck a chord with me. Junior high school introduced me to my first Jewish friends. One of them invited me to her birthday party on a Friday night, where her family lit candles. She told me they burned candles every Friday night. My family had no such religious rituals.

Languages and music interested me all my life. I was 12 when I saw an article in the newspaper about a temple offering after-school Hebrew lessons. The class was intended for Jewish children preparing for *bar* and *bat mitzvah*, and I was disappointed and embarrassed. About the same time, I heard George Gershwin's *Rhapsody in Blue* and *Porgy and Bess*. Enthralled by his music, I read Gershwin's biography and learned about the Jewish immigrant experience. I played *Rhapsody in Blue* at the annual recital given by my piano teacher.

By age 18, I decided I was an atheist. I had just entered UCLA. Before leaving for college, I discussed religion with a friend. My parents had divorced and it dawned on me that the Jewish concept of God seemed more in line with what my mother had taught me a decade before.

Jewish friends took a group of us to a synagogue before and during the Six-Day War. When I received my driver's license, I returned several times on my own. On the first morning of Passover, I was the only one there. The rabbi and I sat in his office and talked about the differences between Christianity and Judaism, and also about the war in Vietnam.

At UCLA, I met Jews involved in the anti-war movement and civil rights, and that's when I made the decision to convert. My mother was glad I found something that made me happy. My older sister and her husband, conservative Christians, ask me to bring a Hanukkah *menorah* to their home in December. My sister once attended a *Seder* with me.

At UCLA, I became involved with a Reform synagogue where I had an adult *bar mitzvah*, after which I taught in the religious school and served as the senior high school adviser. When one of my Jewish professors found out I converted, she said, "I hope you get over it." A shopkeeper in the predominantly Jewish area of Los Angeles, California, always asked me, "Are you still trying to be Jewish?"

After graduating, I traveled to Israel several times. I began keeping kosher, and then decided to seek a *halachic* conversion. I met Susan Friedman, a Jewish studies major at the University of Southern California and what is now American Jewish University, and we married. Instead of hyphenating our name we selected the consonants FRDS from our names, changed the F to a P and came up with *Pardess*, a Hebrew word that means "orchard" or "grove."

Before Susan passed away, we had two children, Rebecca and Ross, who only know me as a Jewish parent. Both of them attended a Hebrew academy, and they became *bat* and *bar mitzvah*. We're Jewish. We celebrate life.

Julie Paul

A S A YOUNG CHILD, I enjoyed the big social event of going to church with my extended family on Sundays. Through the years, the social aspects lessened as relatives moved away. By the time I was a teenager, my parents only went to services occasionally and permitted my three brothers and me to decide whether we wanted to attend.

I had been uncomfortable with the concepts that were being taught there for a while. I did not believe that Jesus Christ was the "Son of God." I felt he was a man like any other man.

I did not believe I was going to hell. I did not believe that God, if there was a God, punished people just because they were unable to believe. I did not accept the notion that all of the other people on the planet who had different belief systems, but were basically good people, were going to hell.

I did not believe there was only one right way to think or that asking questions should be discouraged. I'm a book-lover and one of the things I love about books is the wealth of different points of view. In Christianity, as I was taught it, there is only one correct path. I decided not to go back to church.

When Christianity did not work for me, I gave up on religion. I did not pursue other religions and reject them. I just stopped having religion in my life. I thought, "Who needs it?" Religion helped people to be good. But even without religion, I thought was a pretty good person. I remember being happy when I learned the word "agnostic." I knew what I did not believe, but I was not sure what I did believe.

This was the way I described myself by the time I was in college and met Larry. At some point, he mentioned that he was Jewish, as if that might be a problem. Eventually, Larry mentioned that he saw himself ending up with someone who was Jewish. Although it was important to him, he had difficulty articulating why it was so important.

Larry and I broke up a couple of times because it seemed like an insurmountable hurdle. But we also got back together again and again, mostly because we were good friends. I even flew halfway around the world to see Larry when he was wrapping up a project in Japan; this was while we were still technically on a break.

I asked him why it was important to be Jewish. He would talk about the Holocaust and how vital it was that the Jewish people survive. However, looking at Judaism only in a survival context just made it scary. All of his answers seemed to offer as many reasons not to be Jewish as to become Jewish. The existence of people who wanted to eliminate the Jews was not a compelling reason.

I borrowed a book from one of my brothers about world religions. I read Chaim Potok's book, *The Chosen*. Neither of them told me what I wanted to know. I was searching for answers about Judaism, but I did not know where to look.

One day I saw a catalog from what is now American Jewish University and found the Introduction to Judaism class. I was advised that if I had a "significant other," he should take the class with me. So, both Larry and I signed up.

I went into the program determined not to change. During the class, we read books, attended support groups and explored Jewish observances. As I became immersed in it, I understood what it felt like to be Jewish.

I don't know exactly when it happened, but I came to the decision to become Jewish fairly easily. I made the choice because I already felt Jewish. I felt a sense of peace I had never known before because the world made sense to me in a way it never had.

My immediate family handled the news pretty well and they wanted to know what it would mean. Would I still show up at family gatherings such as Christmas? I said that I would still come. Only now it was their holiday, not our holiday.

One of the things I enjoyed getting to do as a Jew by choice was choosing my Hebrew name. I always believed that names were important, so I thought long and hard about it and did lots of research. I finally chose the name *Israela* for several reasons. The name Israel came out of the struggle between God and Jacob. Questioning God was one of the main things that drew me toward Judaism. Also, some interpretations that I read said that Jacob wrestled with an angel and my Chinese name means "angel." I was wrestling with God, but also wrestling with myself or wrestling the God within myself.

Larry and I married 10 years ago. We have two sons, Adam and Emmet. They are raised in a Jewish household and attend a Jewish nursery school.

ॐ

Every Jew should endeavor to bring men under the wings of the Shechina even as Abraham did.

Abot de R. Nathan 12

Wanda Warburton-Peretz

I'M TAKING A BREAK from four art projects: finishing a *chuppah* for my oldest son's wedding, designing a stage set for a Jewish middle school adaptation of *Hair(s)Pray*, creating seven banners of Hebrew words to inspire a meditative atmosphere at a women's annual spirituality retreat and last, but certainly not least, attending to the details of my daughter's *bat mitzvah*. This is my *bat mitzvah* year as well, since I have been a Jew by choice for the last 13 years.

Years ago, I was religiously uncommitted. But I had just married an man who was Jewish (although not "practicing"). We honeymooned in Israel and by the end of three weeks, my spiritual heart had found its home. When I returned home, I registered both of us in an Introduction to Judaism course at what is now American Jewish University. My husband, Avi, felt pressured at first, but he soon began enjoying the classes.

Halfway through the course, I became pregnant. It was a profound moment for all of us. Avi and I, along with our sons, our parents and our friends – some Jewish, some Christian, and some agnostic – were excited by our announcement. We would be welcoming a healthy little girl into our family, but I had to complete my conversion for her to be considered a Jew, plus get remarried in a proper Jewish ceremony for her to be born into a Conservatively recognized union. So my unborn daughter, Emma Simone (*Eliana Shulamit*), and I went into the *mikvah* together.

The last 13 years have been busy. I transferred what I learned in the class on Judaism to create art for synagogues, newlyweds and homes. I have expressed myself through art since I was a child, but my experience with Judaism provides a constant flow of opportunities to express my artistic creativity. This is my *tafkid kadosh* – my holy task. It is the work I am here to do, my way of contributing and inspiring my family of fellow Jews. I would not be able to create any of these works unless I remained open to the energy and inspiration that God, the source of all energy, channels through my mind and my fingertips. I could not create these things without the support of my husband and family, without the inspiration of gifted teachers of Torah, without the trust and encouragement of the communities that surround me. We are all here to serve and uplift each other. I get to do that, with joy, through art!

Marcy Rainey

"Abraham, our father was simply told to leave.
Go forth from your land and from your kindred
and even from your father's house.
To the land that I will show you.
Lech Lecha . . .
This is the setting out.
The leaving of everything behind.
Leaving the social milieu. The preconceptions.
  The definitions. The language.
  The narrowed field
of vision. The expectations.
No longer expecting relationships, memories,
words or letters to mean what they used to mean.
To be, in a word:
Open."

Honey from the Rock
by Lawrence Kushner

RABBI KUSHNER DESCRIBES Abraham's call from God and every year, when the reading of *Parasha Lech Lecha* rolls around, I admit a certain amount of envy. Abraham's invitation from God was so direct, so clear.

I didn't even know I was being summoned. My turn to Judaism was evolutionary, a process that started with my first trip to the Holy Land from which I returned forever changed. I grew up in a churchgoing family and made this trip to Israel as a pilgrimage to better understand Christianity's Jewish roots.

At Yad VaShem, I came face to face with the stark reality and human cost of man's inhumanity to Jews and was emotionally overcome. From that point on, I felt compelled to discover just what it was that inspired Jews to remain faithful to their God and their people even in the face of death, indeed, in the face of evil incarnate.

All kinds of questions flooded into my consciousness demanding attention: What was this thing called *"Shabbat"* and what did it mean to keep it holy as the commandments instruct? I read voraciously for eight years: Jewish history, Jewish theology, the wisdom of the rabbis, and books on Jewish culture and tradition. I even learned Hebrew.

I returned to Israel, my touchstone, many times. I walked the Route of the Patriarchs, I climbed through the caves of Bar Kochba, I scaled the walls of David's City. I steeped myself in all I could find about concepts, places and people—Jewish, Israelite and Israeli—and I was smitten.

Bit by bit my life was changing. I knew I was no longer who I once was. I lit *Shabbat* candles, ate *rugelach* and *falafel*, and attended *Seders*. I was impressed by this tradition that counsels, "You shall not oppress the stranger," that mutes its joy after the parting of the Red Sea because God's other children, the Egyptians, had been drowned there. And I liked the part where being Jewish was, above all, a participatory—not a spectator—event. Life was not to be lived in deferment, in anticipation of divine reward after death, but rather to be lived in the here and now, with the greater purpose of *tikkun olam*.

And then I experienced *Shabbat* in Jerusalem. starting with the hustle and bustle in the city early on Friday, shopping in the craziness that is Machneh Yehuda market, drinking last-minute coffees on Rehov Ben Yehuda that concluded with a warm *"Shabbat shalom."* Men raced against the clock right before sundown with *Shabbat* bouquets tightly in their grasp. The sound of the *Shabbat* siren announced the onset, silence blanketed the city, candles were lit and family members, fresh from pre-*Shabbat* showers, reunited at festive dinners. There were 25 hours or so of Torah study and goodwill from one to another. Wow!

"Tsav le tsav, tsav le tsav, kav le kav, kav le kav" writes Isaiah. "The word of the Lord was upon them, precept upon precept, precept upon precept, line upon line, line upon line, here a little and there a little: that they might go, and fall backward, and be broken, and snared, and taken."

And so it was with me. I experimented with *kashrut* and found meaning in its emphasis on the preservation of innocent life. I incorporated the holidays one by one into my own life. And then, six years after my first trip to Israel, came a defining moment: The first Gulf War began and I despaired for my friends in Israel and I felt a part of *Klal Israel.* The die had been cast, the case for conversion now crystallized and only the formalities remained.

To quote my rabbi, Harold M. Schulweis, "Jews need Jews to be Jewish." And the most critical part of the process remained ahead: assimilation into the Jewish community here at home. With my rabbis shepherding me through the conversion process and the *beit din,* you could say I had a bit of a head start. Our ritual director taught me synagogue skills and started me on the path of Torah reading in my adult *B'nai Mitzvah* class. My participation in choir brought me up to speed on music and the members of my synagogue reached out, one by one, with great warmth. In a few months time, it had become my *shul.*

I chose to become Jewish, to joyously and enthusiastically embrace the traditions and obligations of the covenant, Torah, *mitzvot* and Israel. Every moment of every day, they envelop me as my spiritual *tallit*–my protective, regenerative, sustaining prayer shawl of life. I am called in Israel *"Avital bat Abraham Avinu v' Sarah Imenu."* But personally, I am proud to answer to simply *"Yehudiah"*–Jew.

Toward father and mother we are commanded honor and reverence, toward the prophets to obey them; but toward proselytes we are commanded to have great love in our inmost hearts . . . God, in His glory loves proselytes . . .

Maimonides, *Responsa* 369

Pete Robinson

I MADE THE DECISION to convert at 19 and have been on a journey into Judaism for the past 40 years—exactly the number of years the Jewish people wandered in the wilderness before entering the Promised Land. Their journey was long and difficult, and so was mine. Their journey was life transforming and mine was as well.

When I entered a small Christian college in Idaho at the age of 18, I had no religious convictions. The class I took in Old Testament changed my life. What I had thought was just "pie in the sky stuff" turned out to be the real history of a people of faith, whose history was stranger than fiction and yet true. I determined to become Jewish.

On a trip to visit my parents in California, I stopped at the synagogue closest to home and announced I wanted to be Jewish. The people in the synagogue office looked at me as if I was out of my mind. The rabbi gave me a list of a dozen books to take back to Idaho and told me to return in a year. I came back a year later. He gave me another list and said to come back in another year. When I returned, the rabbi realized I was serious— or perhaps a little crazy—and arranged for my conversion.

I had no idea that it was almost impossible to enter into Judaism without a Jewish community. At that time, Idaho seemed devoid of Jews. From there I moved to Alaska, where it appeared that many people didn't even know what a Jew was.

After a number of years, I decided that I had to live in a Jewish community. I returned to Los Angeles, California, and married a Jewish woman. Rosalyn was hearing-impaired and became profoundly deaf shortly after our marriage. She had a strong Jewish and Hebrew background, but felt extremely uncomfortable at synagogue because her deafness prevented participation and understanding.

We joined a very traditional Conservative synagogue, where almost the entire service was conducted in Hebrew. I understood almost no Hebrew and felt like a fish out of water, just as my wife did because of her hearing problem.

I felt like a complete failure because, after many years, I had made almost no progress in become a practicing Jew. I didn't know how to practice my Judaism and hid the fact I was a convert. Since many of those born Jewish are in the same predicament, I believed I would not stand out. I became a "closet convert."

Our twin daughters went to Hebrew school and I educated myself by sitting in on their lessons, while other parents just dropped off their kids and left. Both daughters were gifted students. They placed first and second in the National Bible Contest. They went on to compete in the International Bible Contest in Jerusalem, Israel. That event was life-transforming. Until then, I had doubts that I was really a Jew. Seeing my two daughters take the top two positions in the United States made me feel that God had validated my conversion personally.

We heard about a special synagogue run by and for the deaf. My wife became a teacher, then the school principal, then the synagogue president and, finally, the lay rabbi. As she learned and grew in her Judaism, so did I. I became the lay cantor at Temple Beth Solomon of the Deaf. I found that praying with my hands as well as my voice added a kinesthetic dimension to prayer that traditional Judaism only hints at. I discovered that I was literally able to fulfill the words of the *V'ahavta* by binding God's words on my hands in a totally unique way. I felt closer to God's presence than ever before.

My beloved wife died after an 11-year struggle with cancer. I started to go to another synagogue closer to my home for *minyan*. I now belong to three synagogues: one Reform and two Conservative. I have come to realize that for me the light of Torah is found when that light is broken into its spectral colors as in a rainbow, allowing the beauty of all Jewish strands to enrich my life. I have come to realize that as Jews by birth are a light to the nations of the world, we Jews by choice are a light to those born Jewish.

When I pray with my hands I pray with my heart and I feel that God allows me to draw close to my darling Rozie. My journey into Judaism has been a long, difficult struggle through a personal *midbar* (wilderness), but I feel that my soul has finally come home. The arrival at my destination was worth all the hardships of my journey into Judaism.

ﯼ

> *If one wishes to adopt Judaism in the name of God, and for the sake of heaven, welcome and befriend him.*

Mekilta to Exodus 18.6

Kristina Neshama Shafton

I GREW UP CATHOLIC in a very small town in Massachusetts and had very little exposure to Jewish culture—or any diversity for that matter. It was only after moving to California and working as a hairdresser in Long Beach that I had my fair share of Jewish clients.

Seven years later, I started dating a well-groomed Jewish (young at the time) gentleman. After dating for a while, he took me to High Holy Days services and I looked forward to the experience. Traffic was horrendous and we were too late. So we went to his apartment where I lit a beautiful white candle as he said a prayer in Hebrew, which I found very attractive. Then we read from the *Mahzor*—he in Hebrew, I in English. The text moved me, stirred the very core of who I am and what I believe. Tears filled my eyes, and my heartbeat was strong and loud in my chest. We read in meditation, prayer and reverence . . . that's when my heart opened to Judaism. There will never be a High Holy Days service more sacred to me.

As the season's changed, I enjoyed all the Jewish holidays. Everything has so much meaning and purpose, is so spiritual and it just plain made sense.

We were one and a half years into our relationship, celebrating each holiday at least once, and I decided to take an introductory course in Judaism. On New Year's Eve, one week before the class started, I shared with my boyfriend how I thought our relationship had long-term potential. He stated in a matter-of-fact way that he had no intention of marrying me. So we broke up.

I attended my first class in Judaism with a broken heart, yet I was so fascinated to learn about Jewish culture and religion. When I learned about the sacredness of *Shabbat*, I was horrified. Friday nights were date nights for a year and a half, and we never lit candles, broke bread, drank wine or said prayers. We broke up, but we still talked. I made it clear that if we ever married, we were having *Shabbat*.

Luckily, he changed his mind. I continued studying, converted and we were married. We now have two beautiful children who receive a great Jewish education. I sit on the board of the Jewish Community Center and am also a member of the women's division of the Jewish Federation. I bake *challah* on Friday and, as promised, our family has *Shabbat!*

I am home!

William Robert Shafton

KRISTINA AND I MET on the dance floor, and I knew there was something special about her. Of course she was beautiful, but she had a radiance and presence that instantly drew me to her. It took a few months of phone calls and a promise to lend her my car in order to secure our first date. As our relationship progressed, my appreciation and affection for her grew, but in my mind there was always a limit to how far the relationship could go given that she wasn't Jewish.

When Kristina and I broke up, the fact that she continued to explore and embrace Judaism for herself (rather than for me) helped set into play an infinite series of blessings that makes my life and our family's lives infinitely richer than I could have imagined.

Every Friday night, I see the Sabbath flame dance in my wife's eyes and the eyes of our children. Her ever-present love is a constant reminder of how we are connected to a heritage that goes back thousands of years and which will continue for thousands more because of the commitment and spirit of women such as Kristina.

Sally Shafton

OUR FAMILY IS ONE OF those lucky ones that have had the opportunity to embrace a convert in our midst. My niece Kristina has been a role model for all of us as we watch her establish herself publicly and privately in Jewish life. It seems to have come so naturally, as if it was always way down deep in her toes. But we all know that it is an ever-evolving and growing consciousness that takes place. She churns up the rest of us as if to say, "What have you done lately to strengthen your Jewish life?" We watch her in awe and realize how lucky her community and we are to have ended up with that bolt of lightning illuminating our path. There are not enough Jewish organizations for her to support. It is indeed our treasure to attend her events in the Jewish community and watch her in action.

Her road to Judaism was not always easy. The mother of one of her dearest Jewish friends told her, "Kristina, you should know that no matter how excited you are with being a Jew that you will never be the same as one who is born into Judaism."

In time, she sent a letter to the woman spelling out her feelings concerning her conversion and asking for acceptance. The relationship repaired and now this woman is one of her great supporters. Kristina took it as another milestone on her way to her newfound religion.

It is difficult for Jews who treasure converts to crawl into the heads of those who do not treasure them. It is a kind of thinking and rejection that we would never accept if it were being done to us. Therefore, it is a travesty to think that some of us practice this great lack of sensitivity to those who have chosen to be part of our people.

We are honored to be Kristina's aunt and uncle. We are the lucky ones to have Kristina as our own and the Jewish community is fortunate to have her as their own.

And, yes, we will be there to join you for that meaningful *Shabbat* anytime. What can I bring?

I LOST MY JOB OF EIGHT YEARS. Both of my sisters were getting married and I didn't have a boyfriend. Life couldn't get worse. I didn't drink or do drugs, so what was left? I prayed to God for strength and returned to the church of my childhood. I met friendly people and neighbors who knew me when I was a kid in Sunday school. Things had not changed in 20 years. Everyone welcomed me in and I felt a connection.

But the longer I attended, the more I had doubts. Although I loved the choir and the stained glass windows and the happy memories of childhood, I did not believe that I was an evil sinner who only Jesus could save.

Maybe this wasn't the right church. I had too many questions and not enough answers. So I turned to the one person who always remained my sounding board: my mother. She thought going back to my religious roots was a great idea and invited me to her church where I heard the same message: Everyone's bad and Jesus is the only way to be saved.

I became very frustrated. I believed in God, but needed a place for Him. I started going from church to church, listening to sermons, meeting ministers and getting an occasional inspirational message, but without feeling as if I belonged.

My sisters married and I had a great job, but I still had no house for God. If I couldn't find myself spiritually, I would throw myself into work that helped others. I'd always been interested in philanthropic work, so I became involved in raising money for cancer research for children and found that many involved in this charity were Jewish.

I was invited to an adult *B'nai Mitzvah* service and it impressed me. The rabbi gave an inspirational speech. The singing of the cantor and congregation was uplifting and beautiful. When I heard the *B'nai Mitzvah* speak, I cried and wondered if this was where I belong. After identifying myself as Christian for so many years, I found myself moving in another direction.

I soon joined a junior fundraising chapter of the City of Hope and met a tall, dark, handsome Jewish man who took me to High Holiday services. Marc didn't care for the synagogue his parents attended and felt we should look elsewhere. Friends recommended a Reform temple where warmth, spirituality and the friendly faces of a close-knit community surrounded us. By now, Marc and I had become serious, and we began attending services on a regular basis.

I spoke with the rabbi about my interest in Judaism and he suggested the Introduction to Judaism program at what is now American Jewish University. Marc and I became engaged, and as an engagement present my mom paid for both of us to attend. Marc felt inspired to learn more about his Jewish heritage and I enjoyed returning to school with a treasured major in Judaism.

All those years of philanthropic work had a name: *tzedakah*. The reason I did it was to make the world a better place and that, too, had a name: *tikkun olam*. My God had a home at last.

Life keeps getting better and better. Several years ago a Conservative synagogue hired me. I'm not only living as a Jew, but also experiencing every holiday, day-today issues and becoming quite the Jewish cook. My child attends Jewish day school and Marc plays on the synagogue adult softball team. I speak about my experience at American Jewish University *Shabbatons* and its Elderhostel program.

Little did I know that when I learned *The Dreidel Song* in elementary school, I would sing along with my son who owns about 30 *dreidels*. I still can't read Hebrew, but I have the rest of my life to learn. One day, I'll have an adult *bat mitzvah* and maybe I'll inspire someone.

I never think of myself as a Jew by choice, but simply a Jew.

ᘒ

A Jew by choice refers to Abraham as 'my father.'

Talmud *Bikkurim* 1.4

Louise Sperr

I WAS RAISED A LUTHERAN, but I had begun to doubt some teachings: I didn't really believe in the Virgin Birth, the Ascension and all the other ideas I was expected to accept on faith. I didn't believe in a personal God who answers prayer.

My interest in Judaism began with a trip to Israel. This was a real eye-opener, as I knew very little about Jews at the time. I read everything I could find, both fiction and nonfiction. I was particularly interested in the Holocaust because my ancestors are German and I needed to understand how such a thing could have happened.

I visited the temple of a friend, where I fell in love with the music and the sound of Hebrew. I visited other temples until I came to a Conservative synagogue, where I stayed. My Friday routine became a long drive to work, to my voice lessons, to *Shabbat* dinner with my friend, to services and then a long drive back home.

Making the decision to convert does not come easy. As I studied, I found myself thinking: "Yes, that's right. That makes sense to me." I never told my parents, who lived in Michigan. They are gone now and I observe *Yahrzeit* for them every year. Everyone else accepted my decision to convert.

Among the things that attracted me to Judaism are the practices of *tikkun olam*, *mitzvot* and *tzedakah*. I have never been sorry about my choice. I only wish my synagogue was closer to home.

Troy Stevenson

IT IS AMAZING HOW EVENTS happen in life that affect and influence us many years later. Growing up back East, I encountered a lot of racism. I thought I created all the hatred directed toward me instead of realizing racism was the other person's issue, not mine. I would go to small towns in New Jersey to play Little League baseball and would get the "Jackie Robinson treatment," then blame myself for all the venom and hatred.

In high school, a turning point in my life, several things happened. I noticed that there were certain people who did not espouse the typical racial sentiments to which I was accustomed. I learned through time that these people were Jewish. For someone who knows the ugliness of racism firsthand, this was a realization that eventually would factor into my decision to convert. One family invited me into their home, rich in the trappings of Judaism: *bar mitzvah* pictures, *menorahs*, displayed *Seder* plates and the Star of David. Immediately, I asked questions that they gladly answered for me.

In my family, religion was a task thrust upon me at birth. Getting to know this Jewish family gave me the opportunity to see children my age excited about their religion and who wanted to participate in its observance. This was quite a dichotomy from the environment in which I was raised. Last, and most important, I was in a high school born-again Christian youth group. I asked questions about the Bible and the meaning of Jesus' teachings. However, the more questions I asked, the more antagonistic people became.

I did not know it at the time, but the right to question is the foundation for my existence in this world. The fact that Christians did not want to answer, or could not answer, my questions was not the issue. The issue became my audacity at questioning them as well as questioning Jesus and the Bible. I didn't realize it at the time, but it had an impact on me.

As a young adult, I fell in love with a Jewish woman whom I later married. She said she could not marry me unless I was Jewish. I told her I would be a hypocrite (at that point in time) to marry someone and adopt her faith just to have her in my life. I would be living a lie. Then, I recalled my high school years and thought fondly of my first encounters with Jewish families. I said I would look into possible conversion. But if I agreed to convert to Judaism, it had to be on my terms: Judaism would have to be in line with my fundamental beliefs.

I was a political science major in college and knew that a strong sense of social justice, equality and fairness had to be part of the equation. Additionally, I studied Gandhi, whose ideals became the foundation of my beliefs. Then I thought about my pain from racism and remembered the persecution of Jews throughout history. I thought, if anybody knows what it's like to be oppressed, persecuted and attacked for their beliefs, it is the Jewish people.

My love for Judaism took hold during conversion classes. The most pivotal moment for me was learning that not only can I ask questions, but that a basic Jewish covenant is that it is essential to ask questions for the growth and wellbeing of an individual as well as society. The rabbis in my conversion class answered all my questions cheerfully and also admitted that they did not know all the answers. This was refreshing and reassuring, and I dedicated my journey to establishing the ideas, beliefs and practice of the Jewish faith.

Throughout the years, I have held true to my Judaism and have rich memories of my path in discovering my Jewish identity. My first marriage ended after 14 years, as we discovered we were not the same at 19 and 21 as we were at 33 and 35. I married again recently to someone who is also grounded in her own Jewish roots. All the joy and pain was necessary and appropriate. I could not have arrived at this point, believe what I believe or be who I am without all the events that made up my choice to embrace Judaism. I feel that as I grow and evolve, so does my dedication. My journey with Judaism has encompassed the better part of my adult life. When I reflect on my choice and the road I have traveled, I cannot help but think that I had the courage to follow my heart and meet any obstacle to fully realize my chosen faith. In essence, my discovery of the Jewish faith is an all-encompassing and enriching discovery of myself.

کم

> *All who adopt Judaism and profess the unity of God's name are Abraham's disciples. Abraham is the father, also his disciples and Jews by choice. There is absolutely no difference between you and us.*
>
> Maimonides' letter to Obadiah the Proselyte

M Y PATH TO BECOMING a Jew by choice took almost 30 years.
Looking back, it was the only path I could have taken.
Thirty-one years ago, I married Bob in a simple ceremony
at his parents' apartment, officiated by one of the few rabbis in New York
who performed "mixed marriages."

I was raised Presbyterian, the daughter of an atheist and a quietly devout Presbyterian, the granddaughter of a fundamentalist Church of Christ minister on one side and a Christian Scientist on the other side. The main messages I received from my parents were that no one path was the correct one and that religion could serve an important role in moral guidance and a sense of community. My entire family attended my wedding and embraced Bob and his family.

I had never believed in the idea of God as it was taught to me and did not have strong feelings about it. We decided our children would be raised as Jews. I decided not to convert because I didn't want to fully reject my mother's religion. We started at a Conservative synagogue and had our children ritually converted, but later moved to a Reform temple where we might find less conflict with our mixed marriage. Eventually, we returned to the Conservative congregation. There, I attended services and learned some of the prayers. We celebrated holidays in our home and I *schlepped* the kids to Hebrew school. I sensed my connection to the synagogue, but I also felt like an imposter. Should I recite the *Shema*? What did that mean to me?

At various times, I met with the rabbi to discuss how I could convert when I didn't believe in God. Through those conversations and listening to his sermons, I began to understand what God was to me and how completely it fit within much of Jewish theology. Our kids had their *bar* and *bat mitzvahs*. While I was allowed to speak, I could not fully participate. The rabbi went out of his way, however, to keep me from feeling like a second-class citizen and that was incredibly important.

I began an Introduction to Judaism course and it provided not only Jewish history and knowledge, but made me aware I could carve out my own view of Judaism and make it a part of me. My rabbi graciously offered to sponsor me and attended my *beit din*. After the *mikvah*, many of my supportive friends and family asked me if I felt different. I honestly had to say that I didn't feel as different as I thought I would. I think my journey was taken at the pace I needed and the final step was confirmation of what my heart had known all along. The rabbi; my mother; my siblings and their children; and, especially, Bob and our children, and our many Jewish friends supported me. I am living proof of the old saying, "It takes a village."

This is not designed as a testimonial, but my story would not be complete unless I recognized Rabbi Harold Schulweis. Without his patient, kind, profound and gentle guidance, I would not have been able to make this journey. And, more important, it probably wouldn't have been such a complete one.

John Tibbets

The person whose faith is alive "breathes"—
absorbing and expelling, believing and doubting.

I WAS RAISED IN A rural Catholic family of the 1950s. In the orchard-rich East Bay town of Mission San Jose—one of the original California missions—I was taught by the nuns from age 5 on. When high school came along, I commuted by bus to San Jose to be instructed by the Society of Jesus, the Jesuits. By age 17, I had applied for, and was accepted into, this Catholic religious order.

The experience would *unmake* my traditional Catholicism.

To their great credit, Jesuits strongly believe in the transformative power of a thoroughgoing education in philosophy, theology and an individual's preferred course of study—in my case, electrical engineering. The result of the Jesuit formation is not easy to predict. It can lead some individuals back to traditional religious practices; others to radically progressive practices; still others to leaving the Jesuit order, Catholicism or belief systems entirely. I myself left the order several years before final ordination to the priesthood, but not until I had a transformative experience—one that eventually led to my becoming a Jew by choice.

On a sunny afternoon in 1967, I was at St. Louis University sitting in my room reading Paul Tillich's *Dynamics of Faith* for a Philosophy of Religion course. At the time, I believed that "faith" was one and the same thing as "belief"—that is, a person of faith believes what is taught. In high school, we were always warned against secular universities where we would acquire new beliefs and "lose our faith." This isn't just a Catholic assumption; it's deeply ingrained into our language. To "have faith" in something is to believe in it even in the face of evidence to the contrary. For me, being a person of faith meant hanging onto the quite specific belief system with which I grew up.

Paul Tillich, a prominent Lutheran theologian, had quite another view. Faith, he said, is not so much about believing things as it is about being concerned about things, specifically about issues that are beyond our day-to-day crises and joys. Faith means that we make the effort, at least sometimes, to extend our horizon and look further out for meaning. And here was the revelation for me: Tillich said that the way we exercise faith is through both belief and *doubt*. The person of faith – that person scanning the horizon – learns from experience. As we learn more, we may come to believe some things we used to doubt and doubt some things we used to believe. Otherwise, we're not really experiencing the world. To Paul Tillich, a person of unwavering belief would no more qualify as a person of faith than would a nihilist who doubts all.

This came as a stunning insight: Tillich's form of religious faith worked the same way that my engineering thinking did. When confronted with a challenge, such as the design of a circuit, I pushed to examine, question, research and test until I could identify what seemed to me true and useful, and what seemed misleading and discardable.

For many years, I reflected on Tillich's insight. In time, I added a metaphor that helped me to internalize it further. In early languages such as Latin (*anima*) and Greek (*pneuma*) – and, I've since learned, in Hebrew (*ruach*) – the root of the word "soul" or "spirit" also means "breath" and "wind." Perhaps it's not totally surprising – "breath" is a kind of wind. And both breath and wind are invisible things that can be felt, hence their association with spirit.

Applying the Tillich lesson, I came to believe that faith is to the life of the soul as breathing is to the life of the body: It's the animating principle. Believing is like inhaling – taking sustenance into ourselves. Doubting is like exhaling – letting go of the material that's no longer useful and is, quite literally, exhausted. The person whose faith is alive "breathes" – absorbing and expelling, believing and doubting. No one can only inhale and survive. No one can only exhale and survive. And no one can simply stop breathing.

On its own, this insight didn't bring me to Judaism. It did, however, free me to go a-wandering. I reflected on it as I left the Jesuits to explore the wider world. I reflected on it again when I entered a marriage and again when that marriage ended, in great pain, 15 years later. And it was firmly implanted when I finally encountered Judaism.

Twenty years ago, at a small dinner party where she had been invited to "keep the conversation going," I met Barbara. We rapidly fell in love and subsequently married.

I had fallen in love with a Jew. At least in part what I was loving was her Jewishness, though, not having known many Jews, I didn't realize it at the time. Barbara was mentally acute, challenging, aggressive and funny –sometimes to the point of irreverence. Yet she had a devout, even sentimental streak when it came to prayer and to God's power. Her terrific, almost 4-year-old daughter, Rachel, was being raised in that spirit.

In Barbara's company I started meeting many Jews: her family, her friends, her near-legendary childhood rabbi. And once Barbara, Rachel and I were a family, we became part of a *havurah* group and eventually of a larger temple community.

The people at Congregation Emanu-El in San Francisco, California, I discovered, had many of the same qualities I loved in Barbara. They were educated, canny, funny, blunt, aggressive, challenging, devoted to family and struggling with ritual.

And Judaism, at least the Reform Judaism I came to know, allowed me to "breathe" spiritually. Belief? Fine. Doubt? Fine. For Reform Jews, faith equals concern, and life requires the continual evaluation of one's relationship to God and to one another.

I like the fact that Judaism invites interpretation. Take the famous scene in Genesis 32 where Jacob wrestles the angel. Is it a good angel, a bad angel, maybe Esau's guardian angel? The Torah explains none of this. In just six Hebrew words, the Torah says roughly: "And Jacob remained alone and a man wrestled with him until the coming of dawn." No angel, just *ish*: man. And the word "wrestle" can alternatively be translated as "roll in the dust with," "get in a dust-up with" or "embrace." There are plenty of blanks to fill in here.

Similarly, much about the Torah appears indistinct, shadowy, elliptical, suggestive–as if specificity itself is an idol to be shunned. Of course, the ultimate example of ellipsis in Judaism is the very name of God. Even though our human consciousness craves specifics, the Torah tells us, God's name is not for hearing, and God's face is not for seeing.

Would a religion that forbids concrete representations of spiritual beings require concrete professions of specific beliefs? Wouldn't it instead tolerate—in fact require—that our collective beliefs and practices be vague, to be filled in only by the living of our individual lives. Judaism requires spiritual breathing—a life of faith that includes belief sometimes, doubts sometimes and learning always.

While my path to Judaism was perhaps unusual, I still think of myself as a rather typical kind of convert. Like many others, somehow I found I'd settled into a community I recognized and that recognized me; a community I appreciated, shared values with and could raise children with; a community that allowed me to grow spiritually.

Reprinted with permission of Reform Judaism magazine, published by the Union for Reform Judaism.

D ID I CHOOSE JUDAISM or did Judaism choose me? I was raised in a fundamentalist religion that believed that people in every religion but ours were going to hell. The Christianity in which I was raised was always looking forward to "over there." We longed to leave this life and live in heaven. Unfortunately, I was pretty happy with this life and "here." And I just couldn't see that God would send people to hell because they had a piano in their church. I became faithless, yet remained spiritual.

In my mid-30s, I went back to college in order to make a career change. During a class on Buddhism, a professor piqued my curiosity and I changed my major to religious studies. Initially, I focused on Eastern religions. One semester, I had the same professor for two classes: Eastern Religions and Eastern Religious Texts. I had to write a paper that would satisfy the requirement of a research paper for each class. After much searching and discussion, I chose to write about the British leaving India at approximately the same time that they turned Palestine over to the Jews. Having no Jewish or Jewish studies background, I checked out library books (this was just before the computer revolution and online research), and read and read and read. I wrote my paper with a very pro-Palestinian slant.

During winter break, I read *The Source* by James Michener. There was so much in the book I did not understand. But the history of religion and the area had me totally hooked.

The Jewish studies program offered a class in Zionism, from a historical and sociological perspective. In class (where I was the only non-Jew), we discussed holidays and Jewish issues. I began to ask my classmates questions: "Do Jews believe in heaven?" "Do Jews believe in hell?" The answers I received at that time frustrated me. But those are the same answers that now cause me to love the Jewish religion. To every question I received a similar answer, "It depends on whom you ask."

I was so fascinated with the community and history of Judaism that I enrolled on scholarship at what is now American Jewish University in its "Intro" program. I was poor and a full-time student as well as a single mother.

Then I read *To Life* by Rabbi Harold Kushner. In those pages, I recognized my belief in life and the world. The premise that God wants us to enjoy this world and make it a better place mirrored my view of God. Living in the here and now mirrored my view of life. That was when I truly fell in love with Judaism.

And so I chose Judaism. Or Judaism chose me. When people hear that I converted, they always ask the same question. Why did I choose to become Jewish? That question is immediately followed by questions about whether I did it in order to marry a Jewish man. I am single and I did not choose to become Jewish for that reason. It is a wonderful fit and I am grateful that I found spirituality in a religion, and that I live with a religion that teaches that we are all made in God's image.

Ruth's Child

With open arms we embrace
You, our Ruth
Trace your lineage to one who taught us all
What it means to choose bravely.

"Where you go, I will go
Where you lodge, I will lodge
Your people shall be my people
And your God, my God
Where you die, I will die
And there will I be buried.
The Lord do so to me, and more also,
If aught but death part you and me."

Who are you?
Whose are you?

You are our daughter bound
Belonging, believing, behaving
We are one family.
One God, one past, one present, one future, one people.

Rabbi Harold M. Schulweis

Philomena Wallace

I T'S HARD TO FIGURE OUT when my journey to Judaism began. That one particular event in my life where I could say, "Yes, that was it!" Perhaps the seed was planted in my soul before I was even born. (The Kabbalists might have some fun with that one.) But if that is the case, then I think God must have a quirky sense of humor because I was born in a country so Catholic that he might as well have just dropped me right in the middle of the Vatican itself. No, not Italy. I was born in a tiny little village in Ireland where a traveling library van stopped at our school. One of the most memorable books I read as a child was *The Diary of Anne Frank*.

I moved to London, England, at the age of 21 and my first job was with an Israeli shipping company–my very first contact with Jews. One might think that was the end of my journey to Judaism. But actually I got on very well with the Israelis once I established that they were not actually shouting at each other all the time, but merely having discussions. There was something kindred about our relationship and I never forgot that feeling. When the company closed its office in London, I moved on to banking and married.

After my divorce, I moved to the United States. One of my Jewish friends introduced me to the religious school director of one of the largest Reform synagogues in Los Angeles, California, where I worked on Sunday mornings. Two years later, I went to work full time for the rabbis. I was still Catholic, but felt completely at home and loved learning about Jewish traditions and festivals. At that time, I was following a very spiritual path that I found enlightening. I started attending services with colleagues from the temple and they patiently answered questions I had about what was going on and why it was going on.

It's amazing how some things just hit you in life. Maybe that's why we have so many expressions for it: "The penny dropped." "The light bulb went off." Well, my light bulb went off while standing at the photocopy machine one day. Judaism is not a religion, it is a way of life. I was already living the life, not as traditional as some, a little more than others, but nevertheless a Jewish life. I signed up at American Jewish University in Los Angeles, California, and about six months later became a Jew. I had no idea how much the journey would change me and the soul-searching involved. I questioned who I was then and who I am now, and somehow I merged the two.

It turned out to be a wonderful gift. My life would never be the same. My amazing Irish family was so supportive of my decision to convert but was a little less supportive when I announced that I was going to Israel. They were terrified for my safety and did not understand the connection between me and Israel. Instead of visiting as a tourist, I signed up for a program called *Sar-El*, or "Volunteers for Israel," which involves serving in the Israeli army for three weeks as a volunteer. It was one of the best experiences I have ever had. Not only did I see Jerusalem, the Kotel, Masada and the Dead Sea, but I had an opportunity to do something to help Israel and support Israelis at a time when suicide bombers and, of course, the media were pounding them.

Becoming Jewish to me means coming home. It's realizing finally who and what I am. I feel very blessed to be part of a community and tradition I have come to love.

Pearl Nolan

W HEN MY SISTER PHILOMENA told me she was converting to Judaism, I thought: "Bloody hell, she is mad going from one major religion to another. But if it makes her happy, I don't have a problem with it."

I didn't have a problem with her going to Israel, but working with the Israeli army, that did worry me. I worried about if anything happened to her out there, if she got caught up in any conflict. Sometimes, I couldn't get her on her mobile phone and that would freak me out. And I think she used to get annoyed when I said, "I can't reach you!" She may not have realized how much I worried about her, but she came home safe and well and that is all that matters.

Carol Weitz

M Y PATH TO JUDAISM evolved through being embraced, in every sense of the word, by my late husband's family. I was raised in a very conservative Baptist family in Central California, attending church services three times a week and memorizing many parts of the Christian Bible. When I left home and moved north to San Francisco to continue my education, much of that religious practice went by the wayside.

A few years later in 1972, I met my "to become" husband, "a nice Jewish doctor" from New York, who was recently divorced and living in San Francisco. Since I loved cooking, adopting meals he liked was easy and preparing for holiday meals even more fun. His New York family welcomed me with open arms, shared happy and sad occasions and lots of wonderful recipes. His then-teenage son and daughter became my children, too. We occasionally attended synagogue, the first time was for *Kol Nidrei*. My husband was in love with cantorial music and opera, and he sang beautifully throughout the services. I became friendly with a group who planned special events at their synagogue and eventually chaired that committee for several years.

My parents had great difficulty accepting my relationship with a Jewish man. But by the time we married, they mellowed and came to love and respect Ernie. Throughout our time together, I was never asked, encouraged or pushed toward Judaism by friends or family. It just became a part of life and a way of life for me.

During a trip to Israel, I learned that Judaism provides the opportunity to explore, question and interpret the Torah, as well as other writings of the sages. I studied with my rabbi, met before the *beit din* and attended the *mikvah* to complete my conversion. When I was called to the Torah the following week after my conversion, many congregants thought they were hearing wrong. Wasn't Carol always Jewish? My rabbi said I was

Jewish in my past life. Ernie and I remarried under the *chuppah* with all the grandchildren, extended family and friends around us.

I have shared in so many wonderful Jewish life cycles, from weddings of my stepchildren, *britot*, baby namings, *bar* and *bat mitzvahs*, weddings and even funerals (not only of our own but of the extended New York family with whom we remain very close). After my husband died, the traditions of *shiva* and *sloshim* helped us all endure that difficult time.

I studied with a friend and in 2003, we celebrated our *b'not mitzvah* together. The wonderful expressions of pride from my grandchildren were especially touching. I continue to be involved in Jewish life and organizations in the San Francisco Bay Area, as well as supporting my children in Los Angeles, California, with their involvement in synagogue life.

I know that the example of the life we lead, our involvement in Jewish organizations and outreach programs, as well as synagogue activities has led to others in our extended family to choose Judaism and to embrace more fully the comfort and joys it offers.

Susie Mandel, Michael Weitz

OUR STEPMOTHER, CAROL, was in our lives and part of our family for years prior to her conversion. She embraced Jewish tradition and made it her own long before her "official" conversion took place.

Through our father, she was exposed to a Jewish home and Jewish way of life, and slowly but surely embraced Jewish traditions, Yiddish expressions, and ultimately it was her decision to create and maintain a kosher kitchen. The *Seder* meal, the Hanukkah *latkes*, the Rosh Hashanah dinners – for all, she prepares authentic traditional dishes. She became active in her synagogue preparing the *onegs* and attending weekly services.

Carol's values, devotion to family and service to others are principles common to both Christian and Judaic ethics. Carol had more than her share of hardship, but she keeps smiling, doing for everyone, involved in everything. She is the Energizer bunny.

We suspect she fell in love with the Jewish way of life. Dad did it the right way. He never asked her to convert. He was the living example of embracing, discussing and celebrating Judaism. And he won over her heart and mind. We believe her conversion took place long before the *mikvah*.

Carol's conversion was a private affair, not flaunted or promoted. It was not an attempt to please our father or our family. Two years after Dad's passing, Carol had her *bat mitzvah*. She performed proudly and beautifully. Indeed, Carol was not pushed to Judaism. She was pulled to Judaism.

AS I CONTEMPLATE MY PATH toward Judaism, I cannot help but feel that I always had a piece of Judaism in me. I vividly recall going to my first *bar mitzvah* at the age of 13 and feeling remarkably touched by the beauty surrounding the honor bestowed on my childhood friend.

I was raised in a completely secular family with no focus on organized religion and yearned for something more, a driving force that could give meaning to both the spectacular and the mundane.

I looked forward to a time when I would have my own family and longed for something bigger and more meaningful. I began dating Caryn around this time, and I was exposed to a wealth of religious tradition and her warm Jewish family life. I remember feeling "complete" for the first time in years, both having found my ideal companion and the spiritual fulfillment for which I quietly waited.

Tikkun olam was one of the first Jewish concepts that really grabbed me. My first Passover *Seder* with Caryn's family further opened my eyes to the rich culture of Judaism and sparked my interest in conversion. I had a strong desire to learn more about something so central to the most important person in my life and was ecstatic to find a spirituality that I could embrace wholeheartedly. The Jewish religion has an amazing way of affirming what I believe in and that enables me to approach it with conviction and integrity.

Caryn and I thoroughly enjoyed an Introduction to Judaism class. We grew closer and I learned what a wonderful, caring teacher she is. I consider myself lucky to have someone eager to share something so special with me. My journey toward Judaism has deepened my love for Caryn in ways that I could never predict. Our relationship continues to grow stronger and our mutual respect for one another has never been greater.

I appreciate greatly the solidarity and support that the Jewish community offers. The first sermon I heard from our rabbi centered on the topic of conversion and the need to welcome converts as religious equals. He has been instrumental in making me a welcome member of an extended family. His guidance and encouragement aided greatly in the conversion process.

At this point in my journey, I have gone to three High Holiday services and several Saturday services. I enjoy the time I spend with Caryn and her family. The services have always moved me immensely and I greatly enjoy the mental stimulation that the sermons provide. Singing in unison with the congregation makes me realize I am part of something bigger, which is refreshing and spiritually fulfilling. I have also attended many beautiful Jewish weddings, and Caryn and I will stand beneath our own *chuppah* very soon. Slowly, I am learning to read Hebrew and recently took an introduction to Hebrew class through Chabad. Caryn and I also enjoy listening to the prayer CD together.

I have a strong desire to create a Jewish household and hope to instill in my children a rich sense of tradition and mutual respect. My journey is still in its infancy and I am eager to continue my quest for knowledge and study of Torah. I feel blessed to have had the ability to take my time during this process and not feel pressured to complete any one thing on a schedule. I have a lifetime to establish Jewish traditions both for my family and myself. I am also blessed to have a family that is supportive of my decision. My Mom was invited to the *Seder* with Caryn's family and it was exciting to include her in something that makes me so happy. I am also honored that Caryn's mother has expressed interest in sharing an adult *bar/bat mitzvah* ceremony with me, as she never became a *bat mitzvah*.

I still have a lot to experience as a Jew. I can't wait to hang out in a *Sukkah* during Sukkot or attend the festivities of Purim. It's as if I am a child once again, eager to explore the world of Judaism and excited about new experiences and special rituals in which I will take part. At the same time, I feel as though I have already acquired a Jewish identity and sense the spirituality of this wonderful religion infusing my daily life.

Mare Winningham

Mare Winningham is one of America's most highly regarded performing artists. She has appeared onstage, on the silver screen and in countless television movies and series episodes. Her work has earned her numerous honors including two Emmy Awards and six nominations, an Independent Spirit Award, a Golden Globe nomination, a best supporting actress Academy Award nomination, two Screen Actors Guild nominations and a Peabody Award for Excellence in Television. As a singer and musician, Ms. Winningham has recorded three albums and has written and performed her songs for audiences across America. REFUGE ROCK SUBLIME is her latest album of country/bluegrass/Jewish/folk songs.

I N 2001, the instructor of my Introduction to Judaism class, Rabbi Neal Weinberg, was being honored by what is now American Jewish University in Los Angeles, California. I was asked to perform a song or speak at the event, and I wrote *A Convert Jig* to thank him for changing my life and the lives of so many students with his inspired classes. When I sing the song today, I dedicate it to all the teachers of Judaism, the people who carry on the most important tradition in our people's history: Education.

A Convert Jig

Guard your tongue
Love your neighbor
Help someone to help themselves
It's required—It's not a favor
That is what my teacher tells us

Don't be late you'll miss the prayer aerobics
Ancient melodies you need to know
How to sing the holy songs

To add your voice where it belongs
And how and when to lift up on your toes
That is what my teacher tells us
That is what I've come to learn
He had organized the notes for life
And given me the tools to turn
My tiny insignificance into something big
I will be a Jew like all of you and dance a convert jig

Take the time to learn the Hebrew
Celebrate the holidays
Keep kashrut and study on the Torah
You'll reap rewards forever and always

Cut your flowers
Set your table
Light your candles and say your prayer
Then you'll know how you are able
To feel you're Jewish anywhere
That is what my teacher tells us
That is what I've come to learn
He has organized the notes for life

And given me the tools to turn
My tiny insignificance
Into something big

I will be a Jew like all of you
Your tree has grown a twig
I will be a Jew like all of you and never eat a pig
I will be a Jew like all of you and dance a convert jig

Copyright © 2007 Mare Winningham

God.
>Where?
>Not in me nor in you,
>But between us.

God.
>Not me or mine,
>Nor you or yours,
>But ours.

God.
>Known,
>Not in isolation
>But in relationship.

God.
>Covenanted
>Sacred claims, obligations, commandments.
>Above, below, between.
>Healing, binding, saving,
>Redeeming, shielding, nurturing.
>Godliness.

God.
>In joy and in sorrow.
>In celebration and commemoration
>In laughter and in tears.
>In despair and in hope.

Rabbi Harold M. Schulweis

PART TWO

The Challenge
The Hope, The Joy:
Reaching out
to the World

Rabbi Harold M. Schulweis

Rabbi, Valley Beth Shalom
Encino, California

Rabbi Harold M. Schulweis was named by Newsweek magazine as one of the most influential rabbis in America. He combines a Talmudic education at Yeshiva College with graduate studies in modern philosophical and theological thought at New York University, the Jewish Theological Seminary and the Pacific School of Religion. He lectured in philosophy at the City College of New York, the American Jewish University and Hebrew Union College. Rabbi Schulweis holds a Th.D. in theology.

Through the years, he has been instrumental in the development of synagogue programs such as the Havurah Program, adopted nationally, Paraprofessional Counseling Center, Para-Rabbinics, Jews-by-Choice, outreach to the Developmentally Disabled (Shaare Tikveh and Chaverim), as well as addressing issues of Jewish education and interfaith dialogue. He founded the Jewish Foundation for the Righteous, an organization that identifies and offers grants to non-Jews who risked their lives to save Jews threatened by the Holocaust. After the revelation of genocide in Darfur, Sudan, Rabbi Schulweis founded Jewish World Watch to raise both awareness and funds, to protest the genocide in Darfur, and bring vital assistance to victims of such unrest.

The Stranger In Our Mirror: Jews By Choice

Why does so much of the Jewish agenda center around the convert? Why is so much Jewish energy spent on outreach programs, on Jews by choice, on proposals and arguments dealing with patrilineal descent, on the legitimacy of proselytizing agencies and procedures, on the intermarried and mixed married? Why is the major issue shaking the foundations of Jewish solidarity focused on the amendment to the Law of Return—a matter that has now appeared 43 times before the Israeli Knesset–and which again focuses on the convert?

Why the convert? Why the *ger* and why now? The connection is symptomatic of an internal cultural and religious crisis, a *Kulturkampf* among our people. The controversy over the Law of Return is not simply the manifestation of a political power play between religious factions in Israel or in Israel and the Diaspora. The depth of feeling expressed by world Jewry on the "Who is a Jew?" issue evidences an intuitive folk awareness that something deeper than definitions and demography is involved. Consider that this time, even the appeal to the Holocaust, that ultimate argument for Jewish unity, failed to keep the lid on the seething cauldron of Jewish disputation. This time, the glue failed to keep in check the anger and threats to Jewish unity. It was perhaps the first indication of the exhaustion of the Holocaust as the unifying memory.

We are concentrated on the *ger*, the stranger in our midst, because the *ger* has become a litmus test for the character any destiny of Judaism. How we see the *ger*, how we relate to the stranger in our midst, reflects the way we relate Judaism to the world around us. The *ger* who stands on the threshold of our home is a metaphor for our relationship to Western civilization. The attention focused on the proselyte is a paradigm of the emerging cultural struggle. Hermann Cohen wrote, "In the stranger, man discovered the idea of Judaism." I would add that in the stranger, Jews discover the moral ideal of Judaism.

Toward the *ger*, there is ambivalence within our tradition. In the words of Aharon Lichtenstein, the *rosh yeshivah* of *Har Etzion* there is "encouragement on the one hand and repulsion on the other; some esteemed the *ger* while others approached him with cautious apprehension" ("On Conversion," *Tradition*, Winter 1988).

I identify two dominant strains in Judaism toward the *ger*, two fundamental attitudes toward the proselyte that express two basic philosophies of Judaism. At one end of the spectrum is the Ezra strain, named after Ezra the Scribe, who, returning from Babylonia, saw calamity in the intermingling of the "holy seed" with foreign wives whose assimilated children spoke "half in the speech of Ashdod and could not speak the Jew's language."

For the Ezra strain, a conversionary solution for this tragic entanglement is not possible. It presumes that there is a primordial foreignness in the *ger* that cannot be Jewishly assimilated. The unique purity of the people can be restored only by excluding the alienating partner. "Make confession unto the Lord God of your fathers . . . separate yourselves from the people of the land and from the strange foreign women" (Ezra 10:11).

At the other end of the spectrum is the Ruth strain, which stands genealogical conceits on their head and transforms alleged genetic flaws into providential virtue. The ancestry of Davidic royalty and messianic status is doubly flawed, audaciously traced back to incestuous unions with biblically forbidden peoples. On the mother's side, David stems from the Moabite Ruth, but according to Deuteronomy, a Moabite "shall not enter the assembly of the Lord," and the eponymous ancestor of Moab was the child of an incestuous union between father Lot and his daughter. On the father's side, David's lineage is derived from Peretz, the product of an incestuous union of father-in-law and daughter-in-law, Judah and Tamar (Ruth 4:12). The Ruth strain contradicts with a vengeance the genealogical purity of the Ezra strain. The convert is as the newborn. "Whoever brings another person under the wings of the Shechinah is considered as having created him, shaped him, and brought him into the world" (Tosefta *Horayot* 2:7). "A *ger* is like a newborn babe" (T. *Yevamot* 22a).

The Body Revealed

The Book of Ezra and the Book of Ruth are both canonized biblical texts. Each approach has its own *gilgulim*, its transformations. The Ezra strain is evident in the thinking of Judah Halevi, the Maharal of Prague and the School of Chabad. Its most contemporary resurrection is found in Professor Michael Wyschograd's book *The Body of Faith* (1983). A graduate of Yeshiva University and a teacher of philosophy at Baruch College of the City University of New York, and one of the principal Jewish spokespersons in the international Jewish-Christian dialogue, Wyschograd boldly articulates the Ezra strain. Judaism is a carnal election. God chose the route of election through a biological principle. The *berit* covenant of God with Israel does not take place as an ideological, spiritual, disembodied covenant. Israel's election is transmitted through the body. God chose to elect "a biological people that remains elect even when it sins." The Jew is corporally chosen, chosen in the flesh, regardless of his spiritual or moral merit. The frontispiece of Wyschograd's book carries a statement from the *Sifra*, "Even though they [the Jews] are unclean, the Divine Presence is among them."

Those not elected, those not born Jewish, will of course be hurt or they are not of the seed of Abraham whom God loves above all others. And election has nothing to do with the virtues of the person or people. Wyschograd argues a theology of the Jewish body, a metaphysical sociobiology down to the putatively Jewish facial physiognomy and culinary predilections. "There are those for whom their Jewishness means gefilte fish, bagels with lox and cream cheese, or the smell of chicken simmering in broth. Those who think of those things with derision do not understand Jewish existence as embodied existence. Just as the gait and face of a person is that person, at least in part, so the physiognomy of the Jewish people is, at least in part, the people" (p. 26). "Anatomy is destiny," Freud observed. I have heard such arguments, not from philosophers, but from Jews for whom the inability of the proselyte to assimilate is "alimentary." *De gustibus non disputandum est.* The people of the book favor an Ashkenazic menu.

Following the Ezra strain, Judaism is not essentially a matter of faith or ethics or ideology, but a matter of mysteriously inherited traits. The *Tanya*, the Hasidic classic authored by the founder of Chabad, Schneur Zalman, is the sacred text studied daily by the Lubavitchers. The *Tanya's* metaphysical biologism runs throughout the text, distinguishing Jewish souls from the souls of the nations of the world, which emanate from unclean husks that contain no good whatever.

All the good that the non-Jewish nations do is done only from selfish motives. "From the lower grades of the *kelipot*, altogether unclean and evil, flow the souls of all the nations of the world and the existence of their bodies, and also the souls of all living creatures that are unclean and unfit for human consumption" (chap. 6). Within the Ezra strain, pure, impure, clean and contaminating are the critical categories that divide the souls of God's creation.

Still there is a felt embarrassment in the exclusionary Ezra strain. If Jews inherit character, how can someone not born a Jew acquire the congenital virtues by a sheer act of will? And yet there is an unambiguous legal possibility of conversion. Here the Ezra strain feels compelled to put some limits on the elevation of the proselyte. For Judah Halevi, it is clear that "those who become Jews do not assume equal rank with born Israelites, who are specially privileged to attain prophecy" (Kuzari 1:115). No other nation besides Israel knows the true meaning of the *Tetragrammaton*, no other people has the connection with God. For the Zohar, while the proselyte receives a new soul from heaven, it is not of the same caliber as the souls of Jews by birth (see Jacob Katz, *Exclusiveness and Tolerance*, chap. 12).

The Attractions Of The Ezra Strain

If I dwell on the Ezra strain and barely mention the rabbinic traditions endorsing the Ruth strain, it is because liberal Jews are rarely exposed to the Ezra tradition. The books we read, the tradition we select, the rabbis we hear have filtered out the Ezra view of Judaism. But if we are to understand the implications of our outreach program for Judaism, we must understand the Ezra strain, because it is more alive than we may think, and its presuppositions and implications are very much a part of the contemporary *Kulturkampf*.

The arguments I hear mostly contend that the "Jews by choice" are hopelessly deaf to the ethnic strains of Jewishness. This is, I suspect, a more polite way of saying that Jewishness is an ascription not an acquired character, something you are born with, or as one of my patient congregants put it, "Jewishness, dear Rabbi, comes with the mother's milk."

Indeed, it seems to me that the less practicing and believing the Jew, the more insistent the contention that Jewishness is something born into. The weaker the Jew, the more powerful the attraction to make Jewishness a genetic affair.

Ruth followers must understand the heart of Ezra. Ezra cannot be simply dismissed as bigoted or xenophobic. Ezra has no trust in the viability of a community of choice. Choice is too fragile to assure the Jewishness of his grandchildren. He seeks something independent of choice, a covenant in the flesh, a circumcision in blood. *Be-damayich chayi,* "In thy blood shaft thou live," is recited at the *berit.* The Ezra strain seeks a genetic transmission of loyalty as certain as a transfusion of blood.

There is something reassuring in the genetic fixity applied to Judaism. The sociologist Nathan Glazer argues that "the converted may be better Jews than those born within the fold and indeed often are, but it seems undeniable that their children have alternatives before them that the children of families in which both parents were born Jewish do not—they have legitimate alternative identities" (Nathan Glazer, *New Perspectives in American Jewish Sociology,* American Jewish Committee, 1987). Choice is chancy. Jews by choice chose. But he who chooses for Judaism one day may opt to chose out of Judaism another day, or else his child may. In *halachic* terms, the infant of a Jewish womb, whatever he/she may later choose, is irrevocably Jewish—*Yisrael af al pi shechatah Yisrael hu;* no theological or ritual text is called for. But a non-Jewish infant converted before his/her majority can protest the conversion. The biological Jewish infant is safe. He cannot protest and cannot revert.

Choice And Heresy

There is in the tradition a greater confidence in being chosen than in choosing, in choosing because you are commanded rather than choosing out of your autonomous decisions. The election of Israel (*Avodah Zarah* 2b) took place without consultation with Israel. God overwhelmed Israel. He suspended a mountain over Israel like an upside-down vault, declaring, "If you accept the Torah, it will be well with you, and if not, there you will find your grave." It is God's choice, not Israel's choosing, that assures the irrevocable election and singularity of the Jew.

But it is precisely here that the *ger* in our times challenges the presuppositions of the traditional society. The very title "Jews by Choice" challenges the genetic understanding of Judaism and the preference of biological fate over chosen faith. It raises root questions that touch the nature of our identity and the character of our education. Is Judaism essentially a biological affair, a congenital matter determined by the ovum? Or is Judaism an ideological spiritual matter of faith to be chosen? While, formally, these alternatives are not contradictory–for Israel is a community both of birth and of choice–de facto the Ezra and Ruth strains pull at either end in opposition to each other. There are pragmatic advantages for the Jewish community in retaining elements of both, i.e., accepting Jew by birth without any theological or ritual test and accepting a non-Jew as a Jew by religious and cultural decisions. And yet there are powerful theoretical and pragmatic arguments for rejecting the extremes of the Ezra strain that border on metaphysical racism.

Outreach to the proselyte affects our self-understanding. In the conversion of the *ger*, the native-born is forced to confront himself. The *ger* of adoption places greater weight on choice, will, faith ideology. The contemporary calls for greater Jewish "spirituality," the growing emphasis on theological clarification within the religious movements, the disenchantment with mere belonging, all reflect the shifting of the pendulum from destiny to decision, from being chosen by an external fate to freely choosing by inner conviction.

"Heresy" comes from a Greek word, *hairein*, which means "to choose." In the closed society of the pre-modern world, choice was heretical. In the open society, choice has become the noble spiritual imperative. "Modern consciousness," Peter Berger summarizes, "entails a movement from fate to choice." In modernity, the pendulum shifts from Ezra to Ruth. The *ger* challenges the presuppositions that value biological fate over faith, that make of Judaism a theology of the inherited body-soul and ignore the willful attachment to faith, the longing for spirituality.

All this affects the consciousness of the native-born. The Jewish attitude toward the *ger* presents in concentrated form a clue to the Jewish
relationship to Western civilization that lies at the heart of the contemporary *Kulturkampf*. The *ger* is the microcosm of the world outside us.

We are shaped by those we shape. The artist is revealed in his art. The
ger comes to us from the outside and leads us to look inside. In the process
of *giyur* (conversion), the native Jew is enlarged. The *ger* enters a new
covenant with God and us, transforming us, reinforcing the genius of
Jewish universalism. The *ger* who brings *bikkurim* (first fruits) to the Temple is entitled to declare that God has sworn to his fathers to give them
the land, for when God spoke to Abraham He said, "I have made you a
father unto the multitude of nations" (Genesis 17:8). In this sense, Abraham is transformed. For, as the Talmud *Yerushalmi* has it, while in the
past Abraham was only the father of Aram, through the acceptance of the
ger he became "father of all those in the world who ever become Jewish"
(*Bikkurim* 1:4). Through the *ger*, the view of Judaism is enlarged. A uni-
versal community of faith is added to the particular community of birth.
When the *knesset yisrael* turns away from the *ger*, *knesset yisrael* turns away
from the world; turning toward the *ger*, *knesset yisrael* enters the wider
world. The *Kulturkampf* struggling over our posture towards the *ger* entails a struggle over our attitude toward Western civilization.

Ruth, Naomi And Boaz In Our Times

Much of the conflict between the followers of Ezra and of Ruth lies beneath the surface of the *Kulturkampf*. But for Jews for whom the Ezra
strain is outmoded and irrelevant, the Ruth strain presents its own challenges. Who is the Ruth of our time? The Ruth of our era who approaches
us is neither the Ruth of pagan times nor of Christian dominance. The
Ruth of modernity is less likely than before to come to us with church
dogmas from alien theologies. She comes from a highly secularized culture, a neutral society. She seeks in Judaism the warmth of a family
attached to the rootedness of tradition, the joys of festival celebration and

commemoration, the sense of superordinate purpose that can overcome the shriveled culture of secular neutrality. She seeks songs to be sung, stories to be told, choreography to be danced, memories to be relived, wisdoms to be enacted and faiths to be revered. She seeks a family of spiritual literacy and refinement.

The Ruth of modernity comes to us with great expectations. She has felt the shiver of history. She has immersed herself in *mikvah* and study. She comes to the promised Sabbath table of her beloved and to the Sabbath table of her betrothed's Jewish family. The table is beautifully set, but the evening is graceless and without benediction. The conversations are pedestrian, banal, materialistic, hedonistic and indistinguishable from any non-Jewish middle-class family. The native-born family is Jewishly mute. They are pseudo-universalists like those who would "speak in general without using any language in particular" (Santayana). But Ruth seeks the particular language of Judaism. In her adopted Jewish family, she finds no ethnicity of song or narration, no Jewish poetry or ritual choreography or theology. Ruth is prepared to pledge to her beloved, "Thy people shall be my people, thy God, my God." But where are the God and people in the native-born husband and in-laws? Ruth's Jewish family is in most things a neutral soul, living spiritually in the naked square.

The question is not whether Ruth, the stranger, can be integrated into the Jewish family, but whether the estrangement of the Jewish family from Judaism can be overcome. It is the foreignness, the alienation of the Jewish family, not the purported foreignness of the proselyte that is haunting. The Ruth of modernity is not the Ruth of the tradition, and neither are the Boaz and Naomi of our times those of the Scriptures. The *ger* challenges us to think deeply about our noblest intent to reach out. Reach out–with whom? Reach out–with what? And after touching the *ger*, bring her home–where?

There can be no outreach without in-reach. Outreach without in-reach is not only premature, it results in frustration, embarrassment and disillusionment. Outreach must be doubly targeted. It must be simultaneously directed toward the alienation within as much as toward the stranger without.

You cannot reach the *ger* except through the native-born. And especially in Judaism, whose substructure is the family, it is in the private home, not in the public institution, that the Jewishness of belonging, believing and behaving is most effectively transmitted and lived. Outreach to the stranger must be coupled with the Jewish empowerment of the host family.

The *ger* cannot be converted to Judaism as a theological abstraction. The *ger*, like the native-born, cannot thrive in the megastructure of Jewish society. The *ger* needs a sustaining, personal environment. Jews need Jews to be Jewish. The *ger* needs Jews to be Jewish. The *ger* needs a Jewish home. To support that home must be the primary task of our Jewish public institutions. Each synagogue, temple and Jewish center must plan the formation of *mechanchei mishpachah*, lay and professional family educators resolved to enter the private domain, the *reshut ha-yachid*, for the purpose of enhancing the Jewish home. Outreach begins with in-reach. The education of the *ger* cannot be isolated from the education of the native-born. Both need to cultivate Jewish talents, competencies and sensibilities. Therein is the twin goal, the dual task of a lay and professional teaching collegiality. One law and one pedagogy for the home-born and for the stranger that dwells among us.

The *ger* is our mirror. We have only to look at it to discover that the stranger is us. It is a shock of recognition that holds the promise of renewal. On the evening of return, on *Kol Nidrei*, we pray, "And the congregation of Israel shall be forgiven as well the stranger that dwells in their midst."

Rabbi Bradley Shavit Artson

Dean, Ziegler School of Rabbinic Studies
American Jewish University,
Los Angeles, California

Rabbi Bradley Shavit Artson is Vice President of American Jewish University and supervises the Louis & Judith Miller Introduction to Judaism Program, the nation's largest conversion program, and the mikvah at AJU. A doctoral candidate in contemporary theology at Hebrew Union College-Jewish Institute of Religion, he is the author of seven books, most recently The Everyday Torah: Weekly Reflections and Inspirations *(McGraw Hill).*

Just Say Yes

I remember a regular spring ritual I used to practice when I was still a congregational rabbi. The event took place early on a Sunday morning in the spring, as 30 eager people and I carpooled down to Laguna Beach, California. We arrived at the beach looking pretty out of place—me in my suit and tie, about a quarter of the people in loose-fitting swimwear and everyone else looking weepy while burdened with cameras, gifts and snacks. Why were we there? Not to play volleyball and not to bask in the glorious California sunshine. Our purpose was much more sacred and venerable than all that. These 30 people were among the 100 students who had completed my Introduction to Judaism class and were now intent on converting to Judaism. I would gather the crowd around me (including several locals intrigued by our strange gathering). In a loud voice, I would read these words:

God loves the *ger tzedek* who has come by choice more than all the crowds of Israel who stood before Mount Sinai. The Children of Israel agreed to a covenant with God only after they witnessed the thunder, lightning, quaking mountains and the sound of trumpets. But the *ger tzedek*, who experienced none of these marvels, chooses to enter the covenant with God and to take on the yoke of heaven without the benefit of miracles. Can anyone be more beloved than this person?

Then I offered a blessing to those who were about to use the Pacific Ocean as their *mikvah*: You have come to this place, demonstrating through an ancient practice that you desire to bathe in the waters of Judaism and that you seek to immerse yourself in the religion and people of your choosing. May this commitment always be a source of blessing and contentment to you and to those who love you. May your *tevillah*, immersion, inspire you and strengthen you in your resolve to navigate the ancient and endless stream of Jewish life. May you be among those who will tend that stream, so it will continue to be strong and to flow without end. You are Bountiful, Holy One our God, Majesty of Space-Time, whose *mitzvot* add holiness to our lives and who commanded us concerning immersion for the sake of conversion.

After my words by the shore of the sea, these would-be Jews ran into the chill waters, immersing themselves three times under the waves. Then they surfaced to recite the blessing that marked their entry into our ancient sacred pathway, the path of Torah.

That process, of joining the destiny and faith of the Jewish people, of making our special *brit* with God their own is an ever-inspiring story. It takes great courage and persistence to study the teachings of Judaism, to take on the *mitzvot* as personal obligations and to willingly join a persecuted people.

During my 10 years as a congregational rabbi, I helped about 200 people find their way to Judaism (one became synagogue president, another is already a Conservative rabbi and two more are studying toward ordination at the Ziegler School). At American Jewish University, I supervise the Louis & Judith Miller Introduction to Judaism Program, the nation's largest such program, as well as the university's beautiful *mikvah*.

For too long, the organized Jewish community has been uncertain about whether to embrace converts, whether to create access to help bring these wandering souls home. That time is passed. We cannot afford to be indifferent or tepid toward the many righteous gentiles who have allied themselves to the Jewish people – through friendship, through shared interests and, sometimes, through marriage. Conversion is the solution to the challenge of intermarriage.

Such a solution does not represent a modern deviation. To the contrary, the steps of conversion are found explicitly in the Talmud, and the rabbis of antiquity traced one of the requirements for conversion to the Torah. "Hear out your fellow, and decide justly between anyone and a fellow Israelite or *ger* (stranger or convert)" (Deuteronomy 1:16). The rabbis understand the requirement of "decide justly" (*u'shfatem tzedek*) as establishing the rule that "a conversion requires three judges." Building on that Talmudic base, Rabbi Yehudah established that "one who is converted by a *beit din* is indeed a convert; one who converted by himself is not a convert."

Thus the key to a traditional Jewish conversion is the interview before the *beit din* – the religious court of three observant Jews. After a ritual immersion in a *mikvah* or the ocean, after either *brit milah* (ritual circumcision) or *hatafat dam brit* (taking of a drop of blood to symbolize ritual circumcision for one already medically circumcised) for the male convert, all converts must then appear before the *beit din* to demonstrate that they are sufficiently knowledgeable in Judaism and are interested in converting for sincere motives. Finally, each convert must explicitly accept the authority of Jewish law in its totality.

That last requirement is particularly ironic today, when so many Jews who are born to this wonderful heritage live much of their lives without reference to the *mitzvot* and the depth of the *halacha*. While conversion to Judaism has always required (and still does require) explicit affirmation of the commandments, many people who are lucky enough to be born Jewish don't even pause to consider the place of *mitzvot* in their lives.

Several years ago, the Orthodox, Conservative and Reform rabbis of Denver, Colorado, cooperated on joint standards to conversion. Those standards included: 1) commitment to regular Torah study as an continuing process; 2) certain minimal ritual practices (fasting on Yom Kippur, affixing a mezuzah on the doorpost, candle-lighting on *Shabbat* and festivals, regular attendance at communal worship on *Shabbat* and festivals, maintaining a level of *kashrut* (the dietary laws); and 3) acts of loving-kindness, such as giving to *tzedakah*, affiliation and involvement with a synagogue, a commitment to the Land of Israel expressed in a promise to travel to Israel and a commitment to create a Jewish home in which all children would receive a Jewish education.

Those standards were a minimum expected to make entrance into the Jewish people more than just the addition of a new label. Yet I wonder how many of us, born into Judaism, could rise to the challenge of taking on those standards as our own?

I know that many Jewish fiancés or spouses of converting gentiles were dragged to the introductory classes by their non-Jewish partner, only to surprise themselves by falling in love with the Judaism they discovered there. The wisdom, joy and profundity of Jewish teaching aren't easily distilled to children and teens – it takes an adult mind and an adult range of experiences to reveal the light and depth of Jewish faith and practice. Those Jews had been taking their heritage for granted, blandly equating the ethnic garnish of Jewish living with the substance and beauty of Jewish living and learning.

Introduced to the real thing, they found themselves falling in love with *Shabbat*, with *kashrut*, with care for creation and reverence to the elderly, a passion for peace, the joy of a faithful marriage and countless other blessings that Judaism brings into the world. Several of these Jewish partners now find themselves, a decade later, engaged in Jewish living at a level they would never have discovered without being dragged to those introductory courses.

In an age in which people are free to abandon their Judaism at will, in a time when so many Jews are raised without a Jewish education and lack the experience of Judaism in the home, we are all – in a very real sense – potential converts to Judaism. We each face a personal decision, whether to make Judaism something central to our identities and our lives, whether we are willing to grow to make the words of the *Shema* our own personal pledge of allegiance.

Like our ancestors standing at the foot of Mount Sinai, we have the power to affirm the gift that God offers us, or we can spurn that gift. A continuous legacy stretching across the millennia, a wise and joyous way of life that links the generations, a rich relationship with God and a sacred way of life – these riches are ours as a birthright, if only we are willing to accept them.

Perhaps now is a time to rise to the standards of those faithful people – the converts who bathed in the waters of Judaism for the first time *and* those steadfast Jews who continue to act as beacons of light and fidelity by living their Judaism.

Perhaps now is the time to just say, "Yes."

Rabbi Ken Chasen

Senior Rabbi, Leo Baeck Temple
Los Angeles, California

A former composer for television and film, Rabbi Ken Chasen continues to write and record original liturgical and educational works with his partners in the Jewish musical group, Mah Tovu, whose compositions are heard in sanctuaries, religious schools and summer camps throughout the country. Rabbi Chasen also sits on the national board of the Association of Reform Zionists of America, is a Partner in the Kalsman Institute on Judaism and Health, serves on the board of directors of the KAVOD Tzedakah Collective and is a member of the Synagogue 3000 Leadership Network, devoted to instilling synagogues with new vision in the 21st century.

This Is Our Place

Again and again, I have been surprised by the trajectory, the arc that leads a person to choose Judaism. The story so rarely proceeds in any predictable fashion. During my seminary years, my teachers prepared me to escort men and women who wished to become Jews through a comprehensive and carefully sculpted process of Jewish discovery. I was ready with my practical curriculum of Jewish learning and living; there were books to be read, classes to be taken, practices to be observed, museums to be visited, holidays to be celebrated. Armed with my regimen of prerequisites, I poised myself to respond with confident direction whenever someone said, "Rabbi, I would like to convert to Judaism."

But what was I to do with all those congregants of mine who would not make such a declaration? What would I have to offer to the countless people of different faith backgrounds for whom I would be the rabbi? Was I to wait for them to seek me out for conversion? Were they waiting for me to seek them out? Did I have a suitable regimen for them? Was there a suitable regimen?

Just a few weeks into my first job as a rabbi, I was called upon to co-officiate at a *bris* and naming service for a baby boy born to active congregants. This was their third child. The father, Matthew, was Jewish. The mother, Debbie, was not. Matthew and Debbie understood and embraced the reasons for circumcising their son *l'shem gerut* (for the purpose of his ritual conversion), and yet a mother who wasn't a Jew would still raise him. "Perhaps I should offer Debbie an opportunity to pursue conversion," I wondered. "Maybe she needs me to raise the subject." However, I could not bring myself to do it. An inner voice was telling me that this was not my process to start.

Over the course of the next few months, I discovered the distinctiveness of Debbie's Jewish soul. She was clearly the driving force in raising her three children as Jews, but it was much more than that. She was a frequent *Shabbat* worshiper who sang the words of the *siddur* (prayer book) with joyous conviction. She was a regular student in our *Parshat Hashavua* (weekly Torah portion) class where her comments were characteristically among the most incisive (and often echoed teachings of our greatest sages). She was committed wholly to synagogue voluntarism, as well. Debbie was everything a rabbi could want in a congregant. She just didn't happen to be a Jew.

While Debbie and I were still in our early months of getting to know each other, we learned that her mother had died in the small southern town where Debbie had grown up. Very quickly, a spontaneous *"shiva"* gathering unfolded at the home of this Protestant woman who had lost her Protestant mother. The house was filled with leading members of our congregation, young and old, who came to fulfill the Jewish commandment of *nichum avelim* (comforting the mourner). Transfixed by the beauty of this organic outpouring of sympathy, I remained in the house until the other visitors departed. With embers in the fireplace dying down, Debbie and I sat in the living room and talked about her childhood home, her mother's parenting, her small-town Christianity. And then, finally, I could no longer resist the question.

"Debbie, do you ever think about converting to Judaism?" I asked.

"Not really," she replied.

"I'm surprised," I countered. "You're so deeply immersed in our Jewish community. Look at this turnout tonight from our temple. Don't you feel like you just *ought* to be a Jew?"

"It's not that I wouldn't be honored to be a Jew," Debbie explained. "But it doesn't feel right to me. I hold the Jewish people in such high regard – almost in awe. It's such a remarkable heritage . . . such a deeply meaningful history. It doesn't feel to me like something one can rightly choose. I'm proud to live among the Jewish people and to bestow Jewish identity upon my children. I don't know, however, if I could ever imagine feeling as though I am, in fact, a Jew. Does that make sense?"

"Of course . . . that's fine," I said, not wanting to seem like a proselytizing bully, but wondering whether her statement actually did make sense.

Four years passed before Debbie and I discussed her religious identity again. Her connection to our community steadily deepened during those years. The Jewish content of her family life grew richer. Her worship and study practices continued to intensify. She even became a key participant on a task force that created and shepherded a variety of new experimental models for lifelong Jewish education at our synagogue. Debbie's "non-Jewishness" seemed more and more antithetical with every passing year and yet I remained silent about it. Remembering her living room explanation years earlier, I concluded that it would be inappropriate for me to revisit the matter.

Debbie, however, had a change of heart. "Rabbi, do you have a second?" she asked, poking her head into my office doorway one afternoon. "I'd like to know what's involved in the conversion process. I think I want to convert to Judaism."

I was stunned by the suddenness of her request. "When your mother died, you told me that conversion was really not an option for you. What changed?" I asked.

"It's kind of hard to describe," Debbie answered. "This past Friday night, when we were at services, a wonderful feeling of home sort of washed over me. It was during the *L'cha Dodi* prayer. . . . I looked over at Sally Millner (a past president of the congregation and also a regular *Shabbat* worshiper) and she was just singing her heart out. She's there all the time, just like me. This is our place. And *Shabbat* is our time. We smiled warmly at one another, and I just had this compelling feeling: I am no longer *with* the Jews. . . . I am now *of* the Jews. I can't really explain it. I just realized that Judaism isn't a choice for me to consider anymore. I have already chosen it. So what's the process for me to convert?"

As my heart filled with joy for Debbie, her family and our community, I focused upon her question. It was a different kind of question than the one my rabbinical school teachers had prepared me to answer. What *should* be the process for people such as Debbie to convert?

Instinctively, I took my cue from her. "Agreed," I said. "You have already chosen Judaism. So I'm not going to send you to a class or ask you to read some book that you've probably already read. What's the 'process' for you to convert? The past 20 years have been your process. Let's study Hebrew names together and make a good choice for you, and then let's book a date for *beit din* and *mikvah*."

Debbie was overjoyed. And so was I.

Through the years, I've frequently reconsidered the question that Debbie asked me. What was the process for her to convert? I see several elements.

Debbie possessed a set of spiritual, moral, sociological and intellectual inclinations that enabled her to explore Jewish living deeply without the "product-driven" direction of a conversion process. Her interest in discovering Judaism did not dictate naturally a change in her formal religious identity.

Debbie was a part of a congregation that welcomed interfaith families sensitively and enthusiastically. The presence of other men and women like her strengthened her willingness to seek religious community for herself, not just for her children.

Debbie's congregation truly didn't think of her or treat her as a disappointment because she was disinterested in conversion.

Neither did Debbie's congregation seek to make irrelevant her choice not to convert by treating her ritually as a Jew. She was respected and honored for exactly who she was, and this conveyed the message that she would also be respected and honored as a Jew if ever she chose to become one.

Debbie's "process" also included a rabbi who asked her directly—albeit perhaps too sheepishly—if she might be interested in conversion. It would be wholly inappropriate for Jews to pressure anyone to choose Judaism. But refraining from asking at all could communicate some very problematic messages to the non-Jews in our communities. Silence could convey that we don't care about them, that we don't notice them or, worse, that we'd rather they refrain from joining us. It could also convey that conversion doesn't matter to us, and given the research findings that suggest the significance of conversion in perpetuating lasting Jewish identity in contemporary families, creating such a perception would be irresponsible.

In 21st-century America, where social identity categories are more fluid than ever before, there will be an increasing number of trajectories that might lead to the choice of Judaism if we, as a Jewish community, are ready to create the conditions—the conversion "process"—that will meet the moment.

Regional Director, Outreach and Synagogue Community
Union for Reform Judaism
Pacific Southwest Region

S THE OUTREACH DIRECTOR for the Pacific Southwest for 20
years, I have had the privilege of working with individuals who
chose to become Jewish in transition programs during their first
year after conversion in discussion groups, mentoring programs and one-
on-one discussions.

I was there as a Jewish professional to help each individual and his/her
family understand the process and proceed through the stages of conversion. Yet, over and over again, I was the one who received inspiration.

I heard clear confident voices articulate reasons for choosing and loving
Judaism.

Over and over again, I saw a convert struggle to find words to tell
loving family members: "This choice is not a rejection of our relationship
nor my love for you. It is a step that I want to take at this point my life. I
will always love you and our love for one another will not change."

I shared the awareness of a person's moment of feeling fully Jewish for
the first time. I shared the special moment of requesting a day away from
the office to attend services on Yom Kippur, or a conversation about Israel, or a conversation with a child, or a response to a request for *tzedakah*.
The example does not matter, it is often the moment when the person no
longer strives to be Jewish, but when they actually become a Jew.

I observed the dedication Jews by choice make in order to have Judaism
become part of their lives. I remember a young mother saying: "It was
hard for me to slowly read transliteration when my children are learning
to read Hebrew so easily. I really want *Shabbat* dinner to be a part of our
family life, even if it takes so long to learn how."

I worked with new Jews to develop tools they can use to discuss issues involved in establishing holiday celebrations and traditions. Creating a comfortable balance establishing a Jewish home and celebrating holidays with non-Jewish family members can take time to achieve.

So why, you may ask, am I inspired? Two words sum up my feelings: effort and insight. Every time I hear someone share his/her reason for choosing Judaism, I see it through a fresh lens full of appreciation and awe. I hear: "Judaism is centered in this life." "The reward for doing a *mitzvah* is that you have done a *mitzvah*." This appreciation often brings with it the dedication to put extra effort into the process of making Judaism an important part of daily life.

Every individual who embarks on this journey creates a unique path filled with study, search and decision. I have met individuals who knew Judaism was the right path and others who took years to complete the process. Some begin to study and ultimately choose to participate in the community while maintaining his/her religion of birth.

We are blessed to live in a time when we can openly welcome those who wish to join us. We are blessed by people who join us. Their presence and dedication are great contributions to our community. We are blessed by their stories and thank them for sharing them with us.

Rabbi Edward Feinstein

Senior Rabbi, Valley Beth Shalom
Encino, California

Rabbi Edward Feinstein serves on the faculty of American Jewish University's Ziegler School of Rabbinic Studies, the Wexner Heritage Program, the Whizen Center and the Synagogue 2000 initiative. He writes a column for the Jewish Journal of Greater Los Angeles and lectures widely across the United States. His book, Tough Questions Jews Ask: A Young Adult's Guide to Building a Jewish Life, published by Jewish Lights Publishing in 2003, was one of the American Library Association's top 10 books on religion for young readers and a finalist for the National Jewish Book Award. His stories have been published in a number of anthologies, including Sacred Intentions and Restful Reflections, both edited by Kerry Olitzky and Lori Forman. He graduated with honors from the University of California, Santa Cruz; the University of Judaism; and Columbia University, and was ordained at the Jewish Theological Seminary of America. In 1982, Rabbi Feinstein became the founding director of the Solomon Schechter Academy of Dallas, Texas. In 1990, he assumed the directorship of Camp Ramah in California, the largest Jewish camp and conference center in the Western United States. He came to Valley Beth Shalom in 1993 at the invitation of Rabbi Harold Schulweis.

The Spirituality Of Roots

We are a culture of nomads. We surf the Net and television channels. We enjoy French roast and croissants for breakfast, sushi for lunch and at dinner, we "graze." We multitask at work. We prefer pragmatic political leaders rather than ideological leaders. No news story commands more than fleeting attention—a day or two in the headlines, and then it is replaced by the next catastrophe. No issue attracts more than momentary concern.

The theologian Paul Tillich taught that every person has an "object of ultimate concern." He was wrong. Our nomadic culture looks suspiciously upon those too deeply wedded to anything "ultimate" – any particular cause or value or concern. Passionate conviction just isn't "cool." The nomad views ultimate concerns, intimate relationships, deeply held values as restraints, impinging on his freedom. His is a freedom not *of choice*, but *from choice*. And that freedom is his highest truth.

In the stories throughout this book, we meet people who have found this nomadic culture hollow and lonely. They seek a spiritual home, and have found that home among the Jewish people. In the Bible's book of Ruth, Boaz meets Ruth – a stranger, a widow, an orphan – and instructs her: "Don't go to glean in another field. Don't go elsewhere, but stay here . . ." (Ruth 2:8). Boaz teaches an alternative to the culture of the nomad, he teaches the spirituality of roots. A sense of life's meaning and depth attends those rooted in family, rooted in community, rooted in a spiritual tradition. The very name "Boaz" is a conflation of two Hebrew words: *bo*, "in him," and *oz*, "there is strength." Only from deep roots of conviction and concern can we draw the strength to face the struggle that is life.

The individuals whose stories we celebrate in this volume, together with thousands of others who have chosen to root themselves in the Jewish faith, are a blessing, a gift to the Jewish people. They bring the community new energies and creative perspectives; they bring hearts filled with love for Torah. And more, their presence awakens us to examine the depth of our own roots. A wonderfully sensitive woman, a recent Jew by choice, once confessed her disappointment in the synagogue, "Why don't Jews take prayer more seriously?" And she was right. I cherish her question. And I cherish the sense of embarrassment it brought me. I know the words to the prayers; I've known them since childhood. But she knows the melody so much better. That's holy embarrassment. And it is desperately necessary for the future of our community.

Welcome dear friends. Don't glean elsewhere. Stay here and find God.

Rabbi Joshua Hoffman

Rabbi, Valley Beth Shalom
Encino, California

Rabbi Joshua Hoffman was ordained from American Jewish University's Ziegler School of Rabbinic Studies. He holds a master's degree in education from the University of Judaism and a bachelor's degree in English and American literature from Brandeis University. He taught in the Los Angeles Jewish community, including as a lecturer in liturgy at American Jewish University. Rabbi Hoffman serves currently as chairperson of the West Valley (Los Angeles, California) Rabbinic Task Force and participates in the STAR PEER program, a select national program that trains rabbis to lead the Jewish community to a vibrant future.

Why Did You Choose To Become A Jew?

This is one of the central questions I explore with individuals who consider converting to Judaism and thus embracing the destiny of the Jewish people. The diversity of responses and the intense conviction to live a life guided by Torah is truly inspiring. I am most affected by the religious seeker who comes to Judaism after experimenting with many other religious doctrines and discovers the deep wisdom and flexibility of the Jewish tradition. But once the individual embraces Judaism, do we continue to challenge them and ourselves by this question? Are we reflecting back to the one who embraces Judaism the very best of our tradition?

In my congregation we have a community that openly includes people who have come to cast their faith with the hope of the Jewish people. You will find Jews by choice in every feature of this community's life. From positions of leadership to professional staff, from lay educators to Torah readers on *Shabbat*. The line between Jew by birth and Jew by choice is transparent. Nevertheless, we must constantly look inward to ensure that those seeking to learn about Judaism will bask in the reflections of wisdom, meaningful relationships and hope that living a Jewish life offers. Like the windows that must adorn a *Beit Tefillah*, a sacred prayer space to see the world around us and to allow the world to shed light on our prayers, we must reach out from beyond the four walls of the synagogue to continue guiding those choosing Judaism with kindness and dignity.

We experienced one beautiful moment when we welcomed converts to ascend the *bimah* and be celebrated during our Shavuot services. The highlight of the evening was the unfolding and enveloping of those who converted to Judaism in a 20-foot-long *tallit*. The entire community proceeded to dance with the *Sifrei Torah* (Torah scrolls) around the sanctuary. The ecstatic expression of belonging reminded me that choosing Judaism is an act of the entire self. Our community should reflect nothing less than the total dedication to such devotion and commitment.

Rabbi Steven B. Jacobs

Rabbi Emeritus, Temple Kol Tikvah
Woodland Hills, California

In 2001, Rabbi Steven B. Jacobs was the recipient of the Walter Cronkite Faith and Freedom Award for his work in bringing together the black and Jewish communities. He sits on the executive board of Washington, D.C.-based Faith in Public Life and is a member of the Muslim-American Homeland Security Congress of the Los Angeles County Sheriff's Department in California. He is the founder of the Rabbi Steven B. Jacobs Progressive Faith Foundation that works to advance the connection between all the people of the Abrahamic faiths: Christians, Jews and Muslim.

I was a young rabbi in Miami, Florida, in 1968 when a group of men who were members of the Mattachine Society approached me. This underground society–necessarily underground because of the frightful political and religious climate–supported gays and lesbians. Two of the men, Jews, wanted to be accepted into the organized Jewish community. After lengthy discussions and some research, I opened the tent of my pulpit and delivered a sermon: *The Jewish Community and the Homosexual.*

The sermon allowed non-Jews of the society to hear the openness of Judaism, at least the openness of my Judaism. Other religious communities were adamant in their rejection of gays and lesbians. As I reached out to them, several studied the texts, the history, and the culture and became Jews by choice. I reminded these men and women that being a Jew could be a choice, not only as a matter of birth, thus giving them a Jewish future although they did not have a Jewish past.

Over the course of 42 years on the pulpit, I continued to reach out to those who have chosen or to those who have an interest in becoming Jews as well as to intermarried families. There have been virtually no instances where I have had regrets or guilt in my outreach and welcome of non-Jews and Jews by choice. Many years after being open to all, intermarried non-Jews most often decide to become members of our Jewish faith community. As our community let go of its anxieties of "watering down" the community, we found as we still do, that welcoming and outreach does not mean we must require the Jew by choice to leave behind his or her roots and traditions. Asking one to erase his or her past is painful and insulting. Could we ever ask Jews to forget their loving parents and traditions?

We must continue to reach out, give interested non-Jews a chance to become Jews by choice without obstacles, without requiring them to loosen their birth bonds.

"And thy people shall be my people."

Director and Instructor, Louis & Judith Miller
Introduction to Judaism Program at American Jewish University,
Los Angeles, California

Rabbi Neal Weinberg has a bachelor's degree in music from the University of Southern California School of Music and a master's degree in the study of religion from Temple University in Philadelphia, Pennsylvania. He studied at Hebrew University of Jerusalem in Israel; what is now American Jewish University and Hebrew Union College in Los Angeles, California; and was ordained a rabbi at the Reconstructionist Rabbinical College, but affiliated with Conservative Judaism's Rabbinical Assembly in 1988. Rabbi Weinberg received honorary doctorates from the Reconstructionist Rabbinical College in 2003 and from the Jewish Theological Seminary in 2005.

Who Are The People Converting To Judaism?

Let me share what one of my students wrote about her journey toward Judaism:

"I do not feel I am converting into another person. Rather, I feel I am choosing to make a turn, like driving down the highway that is life and changing lanes. It is still the same old me, driving the same old car, it is just that I am now going down a different road. This road is indeed very new to me, and I do not know my way around it very well yet. Before my current exploration into Judaism, I was in no man's land religionwise. I followed no rules, honored no rituals, reckoned to no spiritual authority. God was an instinct to me; a humble sense that there is something out there bigger than me. What I learned right away about Judaism is that to live Torah is to live a life of rules, rituals and constant tribute to the holiness around us, 613 commandments to be exact. In the Talmud it says: Where people truly wish to go, their feet will manage to take them. Jewish life is sometimes a difficult life, the Torah is a high standard to hold ourselves against, but it breathes meaning into our life and brings a sense of purpose and direction that makes the challenge worthwhile."

Such individuals embrace Judaism, and are ready to live by Jewish values and rituals and live a Jewish way of life. These Jews by choice bring into Judaism a group of knowledgeable, observant and committed religious Jews.

Our program includes single men and women who choose to convert on their own. These singles have no Jewish partner and no Jewish family connections. Often people ask whether they are converting because they have a Jewish partner. This is an insult to these people as if, as individuals, they cannot accept Judaism without an ulterior motive, and an insult to Judaism as if there is nothing worthwhile in Judaism to make a single person accept Judaism without another motive. Singles who convert come back to our program years later with a Jewish fiancé and the born Jew becomes more religious.

We must eliminate the stereotype among Jews that gentiles convert to Judaism only because of marriage. Those considering conversion choose a Jewish partner because they want to find an entry into the Jewish community. Many influences in everyday life lead us in the direction we take in our lives. There is nothing wrong with a gentile studying Judaism because he or she met a Jew. But in the end, that person chooses Judaism. I have had couples break up while in the program and the gentile continues toward conversion demonstrating a genuine interest that has nothing to do with the relationship.

Some couples agree to raise their children as Jews even though the gentile does not convert. If the woman is a gentile, then at the birth of a child, he or she can be converted. There are a number of graduates from our Introduction to Judaism program where one spouse is gentile and the other a Jew who raise their children successfully as Jews, celebrating *Shabbat* and Jewish holidays in their homes and providing a Jewish education for their children in the synagogue.

Through the years, we have had gentile couples and whole families convert to Judaism. For example, I once had a Protestant man and his

Catholic wife who abandoned their religions years before and did not want to raise their children as Christians. Judaism affirmed what they both believed and they converted to Judaism with their children.

The majority of students who take our classes are couples. It could be a Jewish woman with a gentile man, but usually it is a Jewish man with a gentile woman. Through the years, I have seen the number of Jewish women with non-Jewish men increase. Jews meet non-Jews in the workplace or in school. Barriers that once made such relationships forbidden no longer exist. Couples who take our program try to eliminate their religious differences. At the end of our program, many of these mixed couples become Jewish couples through conversion.

Men and women from different races and ethnic groups choose Judaism. In the Southland, the largest group are Hispanic Jews, primarily from Mexico, Central America and South America. They may have met Israeli or Persian Jewish men working in the garment or jewelry business. Often Hispanics believe they come from a *Marrano* background and wish to return to the religion of their ancestors.

Asian women from Korea, Japan, the Philippines and China as well as American-born Asians who meet Jewish men in the workplace, constitute the next largest group. African-Americans are the smallest. They want to be Jewish because they identify with the shared experience of slavery and persecution and do not want to be Christian or Muslim, who historically enslaved them. Statistically, most African-Americans who participate in the conversion program are single.

I am proud of those who take our program and go on to conversion. Some have become rabbis and cantors and active participants in their synagogues leading services, reading Torah, and serving as officers in their synagogues and becoming active in the brotherhoods and sisterhoods.

It is important that we in the Jewish community accept those who choose to live as Jews. They will help us grow and survive and their participation will greatly benefit Judaism.

Rabbi David Wolpe

Rabbi, Sinai Temple
Los Angeles, California

Rabbi David Wolpe was named as the No. 1 rabbi in America by News-week magazine. He taught at the Jewish Theological Seminary of America in New York, New York; American Jewish University in Los Angeles, California; and Hunter College. Currently, he teaches at UCLA. Rabbi Wolpe's work has been profiled in the New York Times and he regularly writes for many publications, including the Los Angeles Times, the Washington Post's On Faith Web site, the Huffington Post, New York Jewish Week, beliefnet.com, the Jerusalem Post and the Jewish Journal of Los Angeles. Also, he won a Simon Rockower Award for Excellence in Jewish Journalism. He has been featured in series on PBS, A&E, the History Channel and the Discovery Channel. He has provided commentary on NBC's Today show, CNN and CBS. Rabbi Wolpe has authored a number of books, including the national best-seller Making Loss Matter: Creating Meaning in Difficult Times. *Rabbi Wolpe's most recent book is* Why Faith Matters.

Where is God? I have heard that question from people attending lectures, programs—even services—in Jewish institutions. Remarkably, it is a question heard most often from Jews by choice.

Jews who grow up outside Jewish tradition are frequently struck that Judaism, which introduced the idea of one God, has so many adherents who are uncomfortable with discussion of God and God's place in the world. Jews speak easily the language of community, of obligation, of *tzedakah*, of Israel, of combating anti-Semitism. But the One in whose name all of this survives cannot always be found.

The revival of God consciousness in Judaism owes a great debt to those who have chosen our tradition, bringing with them an awareness of the centrality of God in Christianity. This spiritual shot in the arm has benefited our community enormously.

There are many reasons to choose the Jewish tradition. We are characterized by passionate concern for family and community, an awareness of injustice and a resolution to repair it, unremitting intellectual inquiry, an ancient guide to life and growing souls, and a history that embraces much of the worldwide struggle of humanity for dignity. We also offer a beautiful, ancient and intimate relationship with God. Too often we have forgotten that, but those who choose us seek it and remind us of our own riches.

There is resistance to Jews by choice; some comes from prejudice, some from fear, some from influences construed as corrosive of Jewish life. But I believe that when this resistance arises, it forces us to re-examine ourselves, and directs us to an internal *tikkun*, a repair of our own souls. It seems ironic to say that Jews need to be reminded of God. Ponder this curious fact: The usual answer to "How are you?" in Jewish discourse is *"Baruch Hashem"*–blessed be God. Three personalities said *"Baruch Hashem"* in the bible: Noah (Genesis 9:26), Eliezer (Genesis 24:27) and Jethro (Exodus 18:10). None was Jewish. If they lived today, I like to think they would choose to be Jewish and help remind us of what we already know. A blessing indeed.

Afterword

THE EDITING OF THIS remarkable series of essays ended prior to Passover and recalls the wonderful event as not only the exodus from slavery to freedom for the Israelites, but also as a moment of rebirth for the Egyptians – ". . . a great mixture had gone up with them . . ." (Exodus 12:38). They joined with lowly slaves to become one people. Israelites and Egyptians journeyed into the desert to worship, and together they set out on a voyage into history. Egyptians and Israelites – our ancestors.

Several times Torah mentions the *ger*, the Jew by choice, specifically. If someone chooses to join with the people "let them come forward to do it, and he will be like a citizen of the land" (Exodus 12:48). And again in Exodus 23:9, "And you shall not oppress an alien (Jew by choice)." That commandment is repeated a number of times "And if a Jew by choice will reside with you in your land, you shall not persecute him. The Jew by choice who resides with you shall be to you like a citizen of yours, and you shall love him as yourself" (Leviticus 19:33–34).

The writers of the essays on the previous pages made soul-searching changes in their lives. Each story is different and, yet, each one contains within it similar elements: a desire to achieve a sense of spirituality; a need to find fulfillment; and a yearning for identification not only with a religion, but also with a people.

Not all of those who participated in the creation of this book are strictly observant, but they have become ardent Jews. The hallmark of observance, belief and identity is not harsh piety, but adherence to values and ethics bound within the philosophy and teachings of Judaism. Everyone of the essayists gave testimony that their decision took place over a long period of time and did not come as a sudden apotheosis – a crack of thunder from Sinai – but a steady, relentless march toward understanding. Their husbands and wives, mothers, fathers, sisters, brothers and children held out their hands in supportive understanding that those who searched found a home.

Nachman of Breslov, grandson of the Baal Shem Tov, wrote that sudden change, sudden conversion, has within it the seeds of danger. "We cannot enter the Gates of Holiness with our first knock. God tells us to wait. . . . Trying to advance in Jewishness too far, too fast, can be disastrous . . . we either delude ourselves and lose contact with our inner selves, or we break down when our souls rebel."

The individuals who share their stories with the community have knocked at the door, studied, understood and come to a conclusion that within Judaism they have found a way of life that matters. Their lesson should be a lesson to all who live in this multicultural society. We all have choices. We are all Jews by choice.

Michael Halperin

Credits

Portions of *Judaism: Embracing the Seeker* appeared previously in: *Under the Shadow of Thy Wings* and *Your People, My People: Journeys,* both edited by Michael Halperin.

Introduction by Harold M. Schulweis. ©2006 Valley Beth Shalom. A California non-profit corporation. All rights reserved.

Excerpts have been taken from previous publications:

Finding Each Other In Judaism by Harold M. Schulweis ©2001 UAHC PRESS. All rights reserved

"Reform Judaism" magazine, published by the Union for Reform Judaism. Reprinted by permission.

Poetic meditations:

Discovering Judaism
©2006 Valley Beth Shalom, a California non-profit corporation

Shehecheyanu: The Response of the Beit Din
©2001 Valley Beth Shalom, a California non-profit corporation

Embracing the Jew by Choice
©2006 Valley Beth Shalom, a California non-profit corporation

Ruth's Child
©2006 Valley Beth Shalom, a California non-profit corporation

Between
©2006 Valley Beth Shalom, a California non-profit corporation

Lyrics:

The Convert Jig
©2007 Mare Winningham

Glossary

Most of the following words appear in the journey essays. We have tried to include all possible meanings. Since the words are transliterations of Hebrew or English words, the English spelling may vary.

Amidah: The central prayer in the Jewish liturgy that is recited each morning, afternoon and evening. As the prayer par excellence, it is sometimes designated as simply *Tefillah* (prayer) and consists of a series of blessings, originally 18 in number for daily worship, hence *Shemoneh Esreh*. The name *Amidah* comes from the fact that the worshipper is commanded to recite it standing.

Aliyah: Immigration to Israel. Also, the honor of being called up to the Torah during a service.

Bar mitzvah/B'nai mitzvah (pl.): The age at which a Jewish male is considered an adult thereby required to observe the laws. This "coming of age" is celebrated by calling the individual up to the Torah and with a festive meal. During the celebration, the individual is referred to as a *bar mitzvah*.

Bat mitzvah/B'not mitzvah (pl.): The age at which a Jewish female is considered an adult thereby required to observe the laws. This "coming of age" is celebrated by calling the individual up to the Torah and with a festive meal. During the celebration, the individual is referred to as a *bat mitzvah*.

Beshallach: One of the weekly Torah portions (Exodus 13:17–17:16). This narrative includes the departure of the Israelites from Egypt and the crossing of the Red Sea.

Bimah: The raised platform at the front of the sanctuary, where the Ark is placed.

B'tselem Eloheim: "In the image of God."

Chuppah: Wedding canopy.

Daven: (Yiddish) To pray.

Dreidel: A spinning top used for children's games during Hanukkah.

Echad: Literally "one." Refers to the central Jewish belief in the oneness of God.

Gabbai/Gabbaim (pl.): A person who assists in the ritual conduct of the synagogue; calls people up to the Torah and ensures that the Torah is read correctly.

Goy: "Nation." Slang term used to refer to a non-Jew; sometimes used in a derogatory manner.

Halacha: Jewish law.

Havdalah: The ceremony marking the end of Shabbat.

Havurah: A group of friends who meet regularly to study, pray, and celebrate Jewish festivals.

Irgun: Acronym for "National Military Organization." A paramilitary Zionist group that operated in the British Mandate of Palestine.

Kashrut: Jewish dietary observance.

Klal Israel: "All of the people of Israel"; the concept that all Jews are one people.

Keruv: "To bring close." A program of Jewish education for faith seekers.

Mahzor: The High Holiday prayer book.

Midrash/Midrashim (pl.): Jewish interpretive literature.

Mikvah: Ritual bath, used for immersion ceremony of Jews by choice, as well as for other religious rituals for purity.

Minyan: The Jewish quorum of ten people required for the recitation of public prayers; also may refer to the daily morning and evening services held at a synagogue.

Mishnah: The major rabbinic commentary on the Bible.

Mishpachah: Family.

Mitzvah/Mitzvot (pl.): A religious obligation. (Yiddish) A good deed.

Mohel: The person who performs the ritual circumcision.

Parashah: A Torah portion.

Pesach: Passover.

Purim: Holiday occurring in spring celebrating Esther's saving of the Jews from Haman's evil plans for their destruction.

Rebbe: (Yiddish) Rabbi.

Shul: (Yiddish) Synagogue.

Seder: Literally "order." Refers to the Passover meal.

Shaare Tikva: The educational program at Valley Beth Shalom for children with special needs.

Shabbat: The Sabbath.

Shabbaton: A retreat that takes place during the Sabbath.

Shema: First word and name of the major Jewish prayer that declares that God is one.

Shiksa: (Yiddish) A non-Jewish woman; generally considered a derogatory term.

Shutafim: Partners.

Simcha/Simchas (pl.)/S'machot: (Hebrew/Yiddish) A happy occasion, a celebration of a life cycle event.

Sukkot/Sukkah: The fall harvest festival during which Jews live and eat in a temporary booth, called a *Sukkah.*

Talmud: The rabbinic commentaries on the Bible and Mishah, including law and lore.

Tanach: Acronym for the Bible. Refers to the three sections: Torah; *Neviim*: Prophets; and *Ketubim*: Writings.

Tikkun olam: "Repairing the World." One of the obligations of being a Jew.

Tzedakah: Righteous giving.

V'ahavta: The first word of the second paragraph of the Shema prayer. Refers to loving God.

Yahrzeit: (Yiddish) The yearly anniversary of someone's death at which time the Kaddish prayer is recited.

Yiddishkayt: (Yiddish) Jewishness.

Yishuv: "Settlement." The term designates the Jewish community of Palestine before the establishment of the state of Israel.

Yad VaShem: The Jerusalem museum, archive and memorial site which documents the Holocaust period.